THE RAW FOODS RESOURCE GUIDE

THE RAW FOODS RESOURCE GUIDE

JEREMY SAFRON

Celestial Arts
Berkeley | Toronto

Originally published in 1999 by Raw Truth Press,
P.O. Box 790358, Paia, HI 96779
(310) RAW-FOOD, www.lovingfoods.com

Celestial Arts
P.O. Box 7123
Berkeley, California 94707
www.tenspeed.com

Distributed in Australia by Simon and Schuster Australia, in Canada by Ten Speed Press Canada, in New Zealand by Southern Publishers Group, in South Africa by Real Books, and in the United Kingdom and Europe by Airlift Book Company.

Cover and Interior Design by Leslie Waltzer, Crowfoot Design

Library of Congress Cataloging-in-Publication Data is on file with the publisher.

First printing, 2005
Printed in the U.S.A.
1 2 3 4 5 6 7 8 9 10 — 09 08 07 06 05

CONTENTS

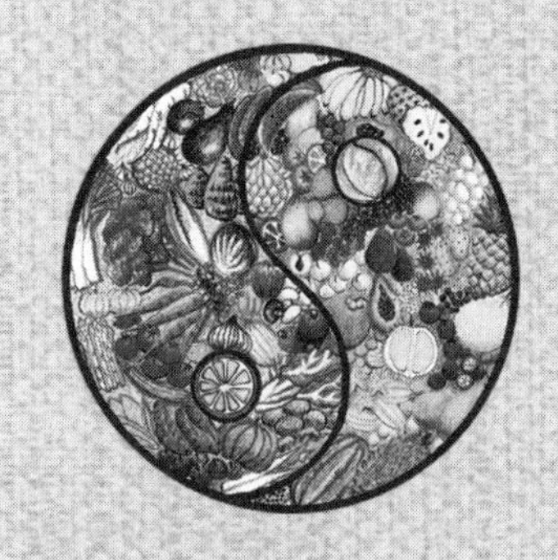

What Is Raw Food?

In the beginning, all creatures consumed their food in a raw form. Somewhere along the way, mankind left Eden and began to use fire on foods. Some people suggest that this was in order to help the food keep longer; others speculate that it was an accident that led to an addiction. Either way, man is now exporting this cooked consciousness to other civilizations and to domesticated animals. Fire is known as a destroyer; if we place an item in the flames, all that is left is ash. When we expose our flesh to fire, we usually get burned (fire-walkers and fire-eaters excluded). If our bodies reach extreme temperatures (above 112°F), we can die. Once man started using fire on food, pioneers and advocates who wished to protect the true diet of man researched, taught, and brought to light all the beauties and benefits of the raw food diet.

Raw food is often defined as anything edible that comes in its uncooked form, referring to anything that occurs naturally. Clearly, fresh fruits right off the tree are as raw as it gets. Fruit is love! To ensure survival, the trees want to have their fruits picked so the seeds can be carried off to be planted elsewhere. We are the parents of the next generation of fruit trees. Leaves and roots are also crucial parts of a balanced raw diet. Many tubers, herbs, greens, and roots that can be found in health food stores are edible wild. Flowers, berries, vine fruits, mushrooms, and sea vegetables are also raw. Most land creatures live primarily on all of these.

Sprouts are also raw. All seeds, nuts, beans, and grains are sproutable, and, in fact, many birds make their diet of sprouts. Fresh foods and sprouted foods are more common in nature, and that is why they represent a greater part of a raw food diet. Cultured foods represent another form of raw food. They are found in nature when the sprouting process is interrupted or when food starts to be eaten by good bacteria. Yet another segment in a raw diet is food that has been dried or dehydrated. Foods can be dried naturally outside where it is hot and dry after a fruiting season or grain harvest.

With human intervention, raw food is much more elaborate. We can create a delight of combinations and plan exquisite meals. One great aspect of a raw food diet is that it is easily prepared and can be radically transformed from its original form. Ultimately, by putting positive intentions into the preparation, beautiful and healthful meals can be created and enjoyed.

History of Raw Food

All living creatures on the planet, except for humans, eat their food in a raw form. No one has to tell the cow to eat grass or the bear to eat berries—they just do it. Over human evolution, most people have been led away from nature and raw food. In reaction, champions of raw foodism have arisen through the years and carried forth nature's cause.

One of the more well known and early advocates of raw food was Jesus Christ. Christ was a member of a community known as the Essenes. The Essenes lived on sprouts and grasses as well as dehydrated breads. Edmond Bordoux Szekley expounded upon the Essene teachings by bringing us the Essene Gospel of Peace (a translation from the Dead Sea Scrolls). Another early advocate of eating fresh raw foods was Leonardo da Vinci. Leonardo understood the relationship between eating well and thinking well. Many people have heard that Leonardo was a vegetarian — not as many know of his writings where he spoke of the importance of using fresh raw fruits and vegetables as the primary food source.

More recently, several people have stepped forward to revive and carry the message of the benefits of raw food. These revivalists include Dr. Ann Wigmore, who in her lifetime brought the importance of sprouts and wheatgrass in the human diet to a worldwide level; Paul Braggs, the originator of health food stores and a pioneer of health through proper exercise and nutrition; Norman Walker, who researched the healing benefits of juicing and brought forth the Norwalk Juicer—a juice press that allows us to get the maximum nutrition and minimum oxidation from our juice and to this day is still arguably the finest juicer invented; T. C. Fry, who expounded the teachings of fruitarianism and helped bring about the Natural Hygiene movement of the 1970s; and

Herbert Shelton, whose teachings on fasting and cleansing have inspired so many. All these teachers have brought to light the crucial teachings of eating uncooked foods straight from nature.

At present, a movement revolving around raw food has emerged. Many people are living in a place that has had the nature eradicated, and they wish to seek it out to regain their health and connection with Mother Earth. Just by eating as naturally as possible and producing as little impact on our bodies (and the planet), each individual is contributing to the raw food movement. Remember, you are what you eat.

BE LIVE!

Benefits of Raw Food

Consuming a diet of primarily or solely raw organic vegan foods provides a large range of benefits. Eating raw food provides 100 percent of the nutrition available to us. The same food in cooked form can have up to 85 percent less nutritional value. Eating living foods also helps us obtain all the enzymes, catalysts that help us digest our food. Enzymes remain intact within living foods not exposed to temperatures above 116°F; otherwise, the enzymes are destroyed, and our bodies have to work harder to digest the foods we consume. Enzyme-rich foods help provide our bodies with a more realistic and efficient energy source. These foods can rapidly break down in our stomach and begin to provide energy and nutrition at a quick rate. When cooked food is consumed either alone or before raw food, it can cause a condition called leukocytosis, an increase in white blood cells. Our bodies may respond to cooked food as if it were a foreign bacteria or a diseased cell, which causes our immune system to waste energy on defending us. By eating only raw food or eating raw food before cooked food, you can prevent leukocytosis.

There are two primary conditions that affect the body: assimilation and elimination. These two functions represent the body's abilities to take in what it needs and get rid of what it doesn't want. All diseases can find their roots in these two conditions. Every ailment is a symptom of either poor elimination or lack of assimilation.

The foods many people have consumed earlier in life have often been less than healing for their bodies, and this can result in a clogged colon. The colon is where we get most of the nutrition out of our foods. At present, many people have their colons clogged with fecal mucoid matter. This debris can sometimes cover the majority of the surface area of the intestinal walls. The walls of the intestines are covered with many folds, curves, and fingerlike projections called villi, which are designed to take in nutrition. The more surface area we have, the more we can assimilate food. When the colon gets overly impacted with fecal mucoid matter, our ability to take in nutrition is degraded.

Many people eat a lot and yet are unable to get what their body needs. A contributing factor to effective assimilation is a healthy intestinal flora (see "Live Cultured Foods"). Eating correct combinations and chewing well allow for greater assimilation. Some of the best-fed people in the world suffer from malnutrition. Fresh raw juice and fruits are the easiest to assimilate. Greens and fibrous foods are wonderful for cleaning out the intestines of old debris. Eating raw food allows for maximum assimilation of what that food has to offer. Many of our true food cravings are nutritionally based. Our bodies know what they need and send word to our senses to seek out foods with these nutrients. In order to absorb the nutrients we seek, we need to have healthy assimilation. If not, we will eat much greater amounts of food in an attempt to get the nutrients we need. Raw food with all of its nutrients and enzymes intact is very easy to absorb and often helps cleanse the body and promote greater assimilation.

Elimination is the process of removing something from the body that is useless or toxic. Many people pick up bacteria or toxic food substances and get ill. This is because their bodies are not releasing the harmful substances. When a healthy body encounters toxic materials, it will quickly pass them out of the system. When toxic materials are encountered by a body suffering from poor elimination, they may get stuck in the system and cause disease. Toxic debris can build up in the body for many years and eventually cause health issues. By eliminating potentially harmful substances, we protect our body and promote greater health and longevity.

There is a wide range of benefits from eating an ideal diet. One of the best forms of life enhancement through eating raw food is the abundant amount of energy that is present. Energy that is spent digesting cooked food can be made free for us to use for other things when eating raw. People eating raw foods find they need to sleep less to feel rested and often attest to achieving goals in their lives that on a cooked food diet seemed unfathomable. Many athletes have found that light raw meals give a more sustainable form of energy and allow them to surpass their previous records. Students also find that raw food gives them a more balanced blood sugar level and helps them think more clearly and stay more focused. Indigenous people throughout the world demonstrate the great life extension benefits that raw food has to offer. Many of these cultures eat a primarily raw diet and live much longer lives. People eating raw food also find it enhances their beauty. Most of all, people who eat well feel good. Feeling good is the essence of life. We enjoy our lives more when we feel good. The Hawaiians say that the most valuable thing a person can have is a positive attitude. By eating well and feeling good, we can be more positive and create a better life for ourselves and those we love.

Four Living Food Groups Chart

Eating 100 percent raw food is easy. It requires eating a balanced diet with certain understandings. Knowledge of nutrition is of great import in order for us to know what our bodies need and to make certain these requirements are met. The body takes in food and will use different parts of it in different ways. The chart pictured below gives a general guideline of what makes a well-balanced raw food diet. By increasing the amount of fresh foods in a cooked food diet, the cleansing process begins and helps flush out old toxins and the addictions that go with them. Greens and fresh fruits are especially helpful in pushing harmful debris out of the cells and the colon. These two primary raw food sources allow a person in transition to adjust his body to eating more and more raw food. As a person feels fuller and more nutrified from eating an increase in raw food, he may begin to experiment with letting go of cooked food. The cultured foods will really help initiate this by increasing the amount of assimilation through proper intestinal flora. The dried foods also assist a person transitioning by giving him a raw food way to satisfy a cooked food craving for something heavy. The chart shows an ideally balanced raw food diet that can be continued through life.

EAT AND BE LIVE!

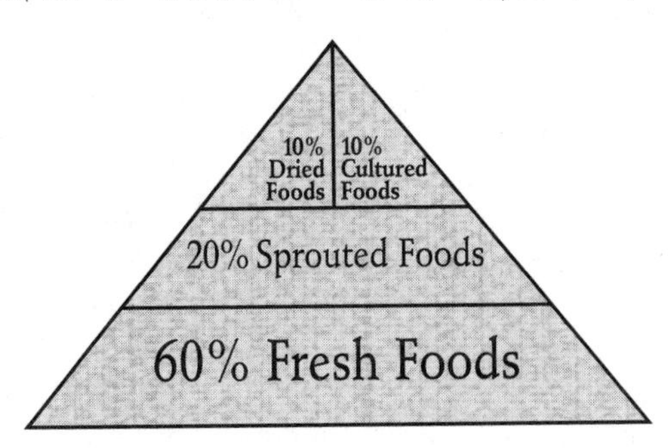

Transitioning Strategies

Each person is unique, and so is her way of eating. In order to transition to a raw plant–based diet, some people may need to take a short amount of time, while others might take years to comfortably shift. People who were raised on a standard American starch-and-meat-based diet may take up to three years to properly transition to a 100 percent living foods diet. Through fasting and cleansing practices, the body can be rebuilt. The cleaner and healthier the body is, the quicker and easier the transition. The four living food groups chart can help structure a transition that is easy and healthy. It is helpful in moving toward healthier eating to work in conscious steps and to keep within your comfort zone. Senseless struggle and self-judgment only impede growth. Dried foods are the closest to cooked foods and can help people who are used to eating bread and pasta. Refer to the information below in order to see the proper percentages that can support transition.

Average American (Poor) Diet
80 percent cooked food
20 percent raw food
Of the 20 percent raw food,
most is dried, and some is fresh

"Healthy" American Diet
60 percent cooked food
40 percent raw food
Of the 40 percent food
20 percent is fresh
10 percent is sprouted
10 percent is dried

A Sustaining Transitional Raw Diet
40 percent fresh food
20 percent sprouted food
20 percent cultured food
20 percent dried food

A Rejuvenating Transitional Raw Diet
20 percent fresh food
40 percent sprouted food
40 percent cultured food

A Balanced Raw Diet
60 percent fresh food
20 percent sprouted food
10 percent cultured food
10 percent dried food

TRANSITIONING TIPS

Change is the only constant. In our eternal growth, we often seek out new ways of thinking, living, and even eating. The transitory period between one way and another can be smooth and easy or quite rough and challenging. The following are a few tips on transitioning to raw food, although many can be applied almost anywhere.

- **Take your time and be patient.** Add and accentuate the positive. Be focused on the good things you ate and did today. Eat the raw and natural foods you enjoy.
- **Start the day raw and see how far you go.** Drink smoothies for breakfast, eat salad at lunch, and start your dinner with a raw soup or salad.
- **Have a raw food dinner party or potluck at your home.** It's a great way to try new dishes, turn people on, and support your new lifestyle.
- **Eat one new raw food each day.** Find out what foods you like and don't. Discover the variety of delicious flavors nature has to offer. If you know your foods, you can create any dish.
- **Go on local plant walks** and familiarize yourself with herbs, fruits, flowers, and greens that grow wild near your home.
- **Dine out at raw cafes** and then go home and re-create your favorite dishes. It is also fun to make old cooked favorites as raw dishes.
- **Always make the best choice** — eat the thing with the most lifeforce and the foods that you know will help your body.
- **Know yourself and educate yourself. Knowledge is power.**

Fresh Raw Foods

Fresh food is any type of raw food that is ready for use in its vibrant form. Examples of fresh food are: fruits, vegetables, herbs, and other harvested food. It is very important to consume large amounts of fresh food. These should make up 60 percent of your daily intake of food. Fresh food contains a high source of organically distilled water (up to 85 percent). Fresh food also contains many vital nutrients and is rich in vitamins. There is a wide variety of fresh foods and it is often best to eat fresh food grown in your own area. These foods represent the element of water, meaning that they are life giving.

Organically Distilled Water

Plants have the natural ability to distill water. A tree will draw inorganic minerals into its roots from stream runoff, rain, and underground springs and transform this into organically distilled water, which it will store in its leaves and fruits. This organically distilled water can be obtained by juicing or eating watery fruits or by drinking coconut water. Inorganic water contains toxic minerals in their inorganic elemental form. These minerals may cause kidney stones and could possibly clog the arteries. The human body does not have the ability to assimilate the metal found in most spring, tap, or rain water. Organic water is held inside the cells of organic matter. This intercellular water easily passes through living tissue carrying in nutrients and filtering out toxins.

Why Organic?

Organic foods are grown without any chemicals, pesticides, or fungicides. Nonorganic or conventionally grown foods may contain deadly poisons that can cause cell damage and toxic build-up and eventually lead to death. These synthetic poisons are completely foreign to humans and animals, and we are just now beginning to see their effects in civilization. Most farms grow sprayed foods because it keeps the pests away, thereby ensuring a larger crop even though the food is deadly. Organic foods are grown the way nature intended with only natural fertilizer that is compost of other organic foods or sea vegetables or plant matter. Plants grown only with these fertilizers are considered grown in a vegan manner (with no animal products). Other organic methods entail using manure and fish emulsion; these are considered organic only if the animals were fed organically.

Seasons of Fruits

Most fruits go from a fruiting season to a dormant stage, to a leaf and branch growing stage, into a flowering stage, and then back again to fruiting. Each variety of fruit has its own internal cycle; therefore, some trees may fruit in the summer, while others fruit in the spring or fall. Some trees may even fruit at different times based on the elevation at which they are grown. Many fruits do have definite seasons, though they vary by geography. For more information, contact your local farmers to verify what fruits are in season, where and when, and start keeping a local seasonal calendar.

Food Combining

Many varieties of foods are available — some that go together quite well, such as mango and papaya, and others that do not combine so well, such as onions and persimmons. For the most part, food combining is intuitive; we do what feels best for our bodies. Some combinations may work wonderfully for one person and not as well for another.

There are many philosophies about food combining; some teachings suggest that it is best to eat fruits separate from vegetables. Some beliefs even advise eating each type of food alone. The main reasoning behind these ideas is that different foods take different amounts of time to digest and some can even impede the digestion of other foods.

Often foods are divided into groups such as acid, subacid, and sweet fruits, grains, greens, and other veggies. People who practice proper food combining try to eat only foods that are classified in the same group. It has been said that fruits if eaten alone take only thirty minutes to digest, whereas most other foods take up to seven hours to digest. For example, melons are best to eat alone. The reason behind this is that melons will be absorbed into the body in fifteen minutes if eaten alone, whereas if eaten in combination with other foods, melons may be forced to take as long as normally required for the other ingested foods to digest. The best message to look for is the quality of stool produced and the sensation the foods give to the body. When foods are eaten in a proper combination, they will feel good and produce no flatulence, and the stool will be solid and will not contain any undigested food particles. Creative digestion is the practice of eating what feels good because the body always knows best.

Juicing

Juicing is extracting the organic water and concentrating vitamins and minerals by removing the pulp and fiber. Juicing is a great way to stay hydrated and enjoy a wide range of nutrition. Juicing is extremely cleansing and healing.

From the Tree Right to Me

Fresh is best! There is a great beauty to consuming foods right under the tree they grew from. Much of the publicly available food is shipped all across the world and is also stored for extended amounts of time. Food when attached to the root or plant is still in the process of growing. When we harvest fruit or other types of fresh foods, they hold their life force for a short time, and then they begin to decompose. The closer you are to the source of harvest, the better the quality of food, and the more vital it is. There are a variety of ways to get closer to the source of growing. One way is to contact local farmers in your area. Another way of obtaining fresh foods is to go to a local farmers' market. Of course, the easiest way is to grow your own. Food that we coparent is of the greatest value because it becomes imbued with our own energy. Interaction with the plants we eat can heal us and help us grow. Remember, you are what you eat!

Cutting and Storing Fresh Foods

When we bite or cut into a fresh food, we rupture its auric field. We are essentially breaking the safety seal that the fruit has. This seal is made up of all the cells of the food, and, when we slice or puncture these cells, we open the fruit up and allow it to begin to oxidize. Oxidation is the process where oxygen combines with other available minerals and feeds bacteria so the fruit can go back to the soil and nourish the seeds within it. All of us have experienced biting into an apple, setting it down for a few moments, and seeing it turn brown; that's oxidation. The best method found for extracting juice from a fruit or vegetable is to press it. By pressing, we cause cells to rupture from within rather than by cutting or popping the cells from the outside. Pressed juice takes up to twenty-four hours to oxidize, while any masticated or centrifugally made juices oxidize in under an hour. Storing of foods is also important. The ancient Egyptians stored food in pyramids. This allows grains and seeds to be stored for considerably longer periods of time. The kamut found in King Tut's tomb thousands of years later was still viable and sprouted. Temperature and light play major roles in the storage of foods. Warmth and direct light make food break down more quickly. So keep your fruits dry, cool, and out of the sun.

Sprouted Foods

Sprouted food is any type of seed, nut, grain, or bean that has been soaked in water and exposed to air and indirect sunlight and, if rinsed daily, forms a new plant beginning with a sprout. Some examples are almond sprouts, buckwheat sprouts, sunflower sprouts, and mung bean sprouts. Sprouted food is often very high in chlorophyll, which in many plants is formed while the plant is in its youngest and most vital stages. Sprouted food is very helpful in building new cells. This food provides the cells with additional oxygen and helps rejuvenate the body. Sprouted food represents the element of air and is regenerating, healing, and cleansing.

The Benefit of Sprouts

Sprouts are potential energy unleashed. All seeds, nuts, beans, and grains are sproutable. The sprout is the young growth of a seed or nut when the enzyme inhibitors have been released and the food has become enzyme rich. Sprouts are abundantly rich in chlorophyll and are quite diverse. Sprouts are a very high source of protein. Sprouts are a high-energy food providing a wide realm or nutrients. Plants know that their seeds or seed-laden fruits will be eaten — in fact, they plan for it. All seeds, nuts, beans, and grains are coated with an enzyme inhibitor. This inhibitor is designed to protect a seed from the digestive system of animals. The enzyme inhibitors are contained on the shell and skin of a seed, and, when eaten whole and raw, the seed can pass through the entire digestive system whole and be planted in a pile of fertilizer to grow a new plant. The best way to release the enzyme inhibitor is to sprout the seed or grind it into a powder. When we grind a seed, we are able to digest it mostly because we have created a greater surface area and broken through the enzyme inhibitor–coated skin. Chewing well is a great way to grind seeds. Sprouting completely releases the enzyme inhibitor and also activates the seeds. Soaking a seed for fifteen minutes releases up to 50 percent of the enzyme inhibitors. The recommended soaking time is for maximum enzyme inhibitor release. Sprouted seeds also have more nutrition than their dry predecessors. Some types of sprouts have as much as five times their original nutritional value. A sprout is the baby plant, so it puts an enormous amount of energy into getting those first few leaves out. The sprouting cycle of a plant's life is where it has the most concentrated nutrition. This is because the sprout wants to become a plant and it knows that it must get a root in the ground and a leaf up to the sky. Once rooted, survival will be much easier. Much like all creatures, sprouts go through their most rapid development at this early stage. The equivalent in humans would be learning to walk or talk; for a sprout, it is creating a wide range of enzymes and vitamins and minerals to get a good start in life. The young sprouts and grasses contain the highest amount of chlorophyll that the plant will ever attain. Sprouts are very nutritious and have many rejuvenating benefits.

Chlorophyll

Chlorophyll is liquid life. All plant life is based upon it. Plants use chlorophyll to transform sunlight and CO^2 into sugar and oxygen. The chlorophyll cell and the human red blood cell are molecularly almost identical.

When ingested, chlorophyll is almost instantly absorbed into the body and feeds abundant amounts of oxygen to the blood, brain, organs, and all cells, allowing them to function at an optimal level. It creates an unfriendly environment for harmful bacteria, helping to protect the body from viruses and infections. Chlorophyll helps build the immune system, detoxifies the organs and cells of the body, cleanses the liver of accumulated toxic oils, and aids in healing wounds. Chlorophyll helps protect cells from the harmful effects of radiation from electricity substations, television, computers, X-rays, nuclear power plants, and nuclear waste. Chlorophyll can be found in all green plants, and specific plants such as wheatgrass contain as much as 70 percent chlorophyll and heal wounds extremely quickly. Sprouting seeds begin the production of chlorophyll using light and water to create life. Chlorophyll-rich food is high in vital enzymes and in B vitamins. Chlorophyll is a healer, protector, and revitalizer. It increases cell growth and thereby helps the body regenerate. Young grasses and sprouts contain some of the highest sources of chlorophyll. Chlorophyll is destroyed by heat. A temperature of greater than 108°F begins to break down the chlorophyll in plants. The greater the temperature, the more quickly the chlorophyll is destroyed. Therefore, food rich in chlorophyll should be eaten raw and not cooked.

Sprouting

Sprouting is the easiest way to grow foods for yourself. You can grow sprouts in any climate anywhere in the world. If you can live there, so can sprouts. You can even sprout in cities right on your windowsill. Sprouting can be accomplished in a variety of ways. You can use a jar method or you can soak your seeds in a cloth bag or even a wicker basket. To sprout, first select the type of seed you wish to grow and refer to the chart on page 23 to find out how long to soak it. Soak the seed. Six to twelve hours later, drain the sprouts. Then rinse the sprouts at least twice a day until the tails are at least three times the size of the seed in length. Next, expose your sprouts to sunlight for about fifteen minutes to activate the abundance of chlorophyll. Now chow down!

SPROUTING TIPS

The length of sprouting time may vary based on climate.

- Sprout time is from drain time to time of consumption.
- Amounts are for half-gallon jar or two-quart sprout bag.
- If using the jar method, it is important to set the jar at a 45° angle. This promotes the maximum amount of drainage and an ideal amount of airflow.
- Make sure the sprouts can breathe — use wide-mouth jars whenever possible.
- Sprouts can drown! Be conscious of the soaking time.
- Buckwheat and sunflower are best when planted like wheatgrass in soil and grown into tasty greens.
- Always rinse with filtered water to promote clean sprouts.

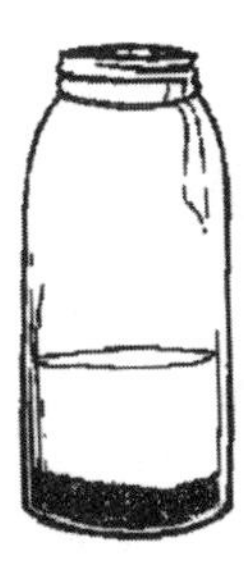
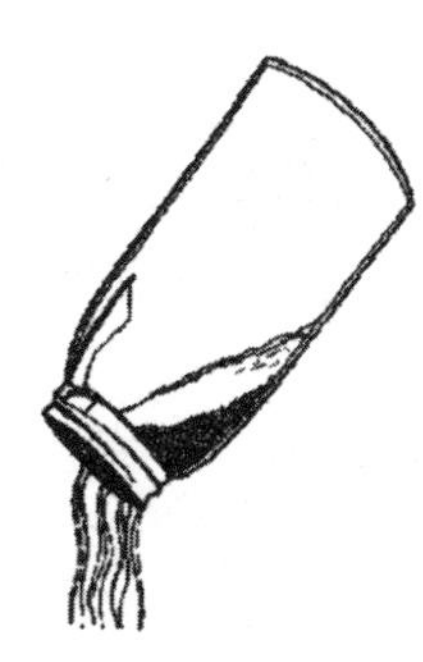

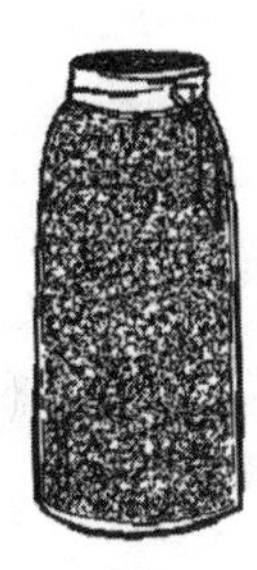

How to Grow Wheatgrass

Wheatgrass is fun and easy to grow. Just follow the sprouting directions on the Sprout Chart for sprouting wheat (page 23) and then spread a thick layer of wheat sprouts on the surface of a tray filled with soil or spread the sprouts on the ground. Then cover the sprouts with a thin layer of soil. Next, cover the tray with mesh or another tray. Water the wheatgrass every day, and after three days it will push up the top tray. Remove the tray and continue to water as needed. When the grass is about 5 inches tall, expose it to sunlight for a few hours to help enrich the chlorophyll. Wheatgrass is one of the highest sources of chlorophyll, containing as much as 70 percent chlorophyll.

There are many varieties of wheat, and all have different purposes. The winter wheat is better for wheatgrass, the soft spring is best for fermenting, and the summer is nice for dehydration and cereal. Wheat has been around for a long time as a staple grain.

It is said that the Essenes had known the abundant value of the benefits of the grass and grew it as a food and lived healthily. Dr. Ann Wigmore has helped enlighten the world to the benefits of wheatgrass. Dr. Ann helped many people overcome their disease and move into a more living foods lifestyle.

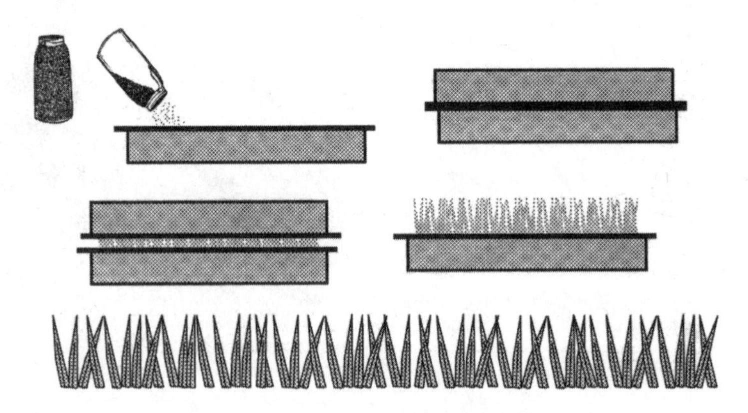

SPROUT CHART

Type of Seed	Soak Time	Sprout Time
Aduki	8 hours	3 days
Alfalfa	6 hours	3 days
Almond	8 hours	1 to 2 days
Buckwheat	6 hours	2 days
Cabbage	6 hours	3 days
Cashew	6 hours	2 days
Chia	5 hours	2 to 3 days
Corn	8 to 10 hours	3 days
Dill	5 hours	2 days
Fenugreek	7 hours	3 days
Flax	6 hours	2 to 3 days
Garbanzo	8 hours	2 to 3 days
Lentil	7 hours	3 days
Macadamia	5 to 7 hours	4 days
Millet	8 hours	3 days
Mung bean	8 hours	3 days
Mustard	6 hours	2 days
Oat groats	6 hours	2 days
Peas	7 hours	3 days
Quinoa	7 hours	2 to 3 days
Radish	6 hours	3 days
Red clover	6 hours	3 days
Rye	8 hours	3 days
Sesame	6 hours	2 days
Soy	8 hours	3 days
Sunflower	7 hours	2 days
Triticale	6 hours	3 days
Wheat	7 hours	2 to 3 days
Wild rice	9 hours	3 to 5 days

Live Cultured Foods

Cultured food is any type of food that has friendly bacteria in it. These cultures live on this food and digest it completely. Cultured foods are filled with enzymes and living bacteria that are extremely necessary for good assimilation. These bacteria, once inside our intestines, deconstruct food and hand us the vital parts. Higher concentration of good bacteria allows for maximum absorption and faster assimilation. A strong concentration of friendly bacteria will also maintain a healthy balance within the intestines and will not leave room for unfriendly bacteria to grow. Cultured food represents the element of fire and is energizing and protecting.

What Are Cultured Foods?

Cultured foods are a type of food that has been predigested by a helpful bacteria such as acidophilus, bifodus, or koji. These cultures are highly beneficial to the body. Live cultures reside on the villi, small fingerlike projections that extend from the intestinal walls. The greater the surface area of the villi, the more room for healthy cultures to live there. The helpful bacteria that now reside in our bodies originally got there through our mother's milk (if we were breast-fed). Cultured foods are live foods. Some cultured foods may have lived on a cooked product. These foods, such as miso, contain none of the original cooked food, only the live raw culture (unless they are pasteurized, in which case the culture is cooked). Many cultured foods live on raw food and are considered both raw and live. These are the most ideal. Some cultures are even grown on sprouts and are extremely excellent tasting and good for us.

What Do Cultured Foods Do for Us?

Cultured foods both protect us from foreign bacteria and energize us through proper assimilation. These helpful bacteria, such as acidophilus, allow for high rates of assimilation of nutrients from our food. Cultures such as acidophilus also act as a protective barrier against harmful cultures that may seek to invade the body. By eating cultured foods, we can increase the strength of our immune system as well as the amount of nutrient absorption in the body. New cultures, both helpful and harmful, enter into the system through the foods we eat. When we create an ideal healthy environment for positive cultures, they grow and proliferate. The same is true for unhealthy cultures when we create an unhealthy environment in our colon. Healthy cultures protect us from disease by standing guard in the intestines and ushering harmful cultures on their way. Often, cleansing practices such as colonics or enemas can wash away health-giving bacteria along with the fecal mucoid matter impacted on the colon. It is important to continually reintroduce healthy bacteria into the system both orally and rectally when following a colon therapy program. Fasting can also deplete the active cultures living in our system, so it is important after long water or dry fasts to reintroduce cultures into the system.

How to Culture Food

Cultured foods can be created by obtaining a starter or by creating the ideal environment for healthy cultures to begin to grow. Often airborne cultures are present, and there is no need for a starter. The starter is a great method for being certain to obtain the correct flavor and is the preferred method. A starter is an already cultured food. Unpasteurized kim chee or miso can be your starter for making your own batch.

STARTER METHOD

(example: kim chee)

Grind or chop 1 to 3 heads of cabbage.

Add 1/4 cup of caraway seeds.

Add 3 crushed cloves of garlic.

Add the juice of 5 lemons.

Add 1 tablespoon of a previous batch of
kim chee or 1 teaspoon live acidophilus culture.

Place in Harsch crock or in glass bowls 5 to 30 days
(some kim chee is aged for months).

A Harsch crock is obtainable through Loving Foods or your local Asian distributor. It is an earthen crock that has a V-ring seal on the top. This means that the mouth of the crock is fluted and water sits in the ringed V-shape and the lid sits in the groove of the V, thereby sealing the crock and its contents. Air goes out but not in. For more cultured food recipes see my book The Raw Truth (Ten Speed Press, 2003).

THE AIRBORNE JAR METHOD

(example: rejuvelak)

Soak 1 cup of quinoa in a half-gallon jar for eight hours.

Drain and rinse the seeds twice daily.

After 24 hours, grind seeds with 6 cups of fresh water
and place in a half-gallon jar.

Let it sit for 12 hours. Drain off the rejuvelak and compost
the seed pulp.

Refrigerate and enjoy. (Reminder: if it smells too
pungent, don't eat it. It should smell lemony).

Where to Obtain Cultures

Cultures can be obtained through a variety of sources. Purchase a previously made cultured food product from your local retail store or contact a health product distributor. These cultured products contain the mother or starter and can be used to create your own cultured foods at home. Some common cultured products available are:

- Seed Cheez from Mount Shasta Rejuvenating Foods
- Kim Chee from Rejuvenative Foods
- Sauerkraut from Fermentations
- Live Apple Cider Vinegar from Braggs
- Sauerkraut from Cultured
- Kombucha mushrooms (get them from friends)

Cultures can also be purchased in their whole form (not on a substance). These are usually sold dry as a powder or as a liquid. Try to get cultures that are growing on something, because they are usually heartier and are specific to what you want to make. When buying a starter, make certain that it is refrigerated. Cultured foods are very temperature sensitive and will no longer be viable if exposed to extreme heat or cold. Here is a good source or live cultures through mail order:

Gold Mine Natural Foods
7805 Arjons Drive
San Diego, CA 92126
(800) 862-2347

Dehydrated Foods

Dehydrated food is any type of food that has had the water removed from it. These foods are very concentrated. Since the water has been removed and the mass of the food has been decreased, dehydrated food allows the intake of greater quantities of nutrients and leaves an intensified version of the food. Dried foods are considered alive only if they were dehydrated below 108°F (the point where enzymes begin to die and minerals and vitamins are denatured). Most dried foods have a longer nutrient retention time due to the lack of oxidation caused by water trapped in the cells. Dried foods can also be rehydrated. Dried food represents the element of earth and is very grounding and sustaining.

The Value of Dried Foods

Dried foods are concentrated nutrition. Most foods can be easily dehydrated by evaporating the water (which makes up anywhere from 30 to 85 percent of the fresh food). A fresh apple that might take us twenty bites to eat takes only three to seven bites to eat dried. Most nuts and seeds are sold dried to create longer stability of the oils. Sea vegetables, fruits, and vegetables are dried for storage. Oils are considered a dried food because they come from a dried seed or nut. Spirulina is also a dried food. In fact, many South American tribes would sun dry spirulina into patties in order to carry the nutrient-rich dried food with them on their long journey across the Andes Mountains.

Dried foods give us a wide range of concentrated minerals and vitamins and a concentrated amount of protein. Dried foods also slow down the metabolism in order to maximize assimilation. The body will rehydrate the dried food and take its time digesting it. Dried foods can be very grounding. Often people transitioning to a raw diet find that they constantly want food. Dried foods will easily fill this need by slowing the digestion and allowing for maximum absorption of both the dried food and other foods that are also in the body. Dried foods can be especially helpful to people who are transitioning to raw food and are used to eating a lot of starchy cooked food.

Methods of Dehydrating

Drying food can be accomplished in a number of ways. One of the most ancient and free ways is to place the food you want to dry in thin layers on a ceramic or glass tray in the sun. Another sun-drying method is to hang a hammock made of mesh or screen outside and put the food to be dried on it. It can be helpful when using these outdoor methods to cover the food with screen and put it in a hard-to-reach spot to prevent other appreciators of drying food from getting to it. Building a solar or home dehydrator is a great project and a simple way to dry food. Buying a commercial or home dehydration unit is often the easiest and most guaranteed way of drying food. The basics are: expose food to 108°F or less until the ideal texture and dryness are obtained. For suggested times, see drying chart.

Kissed by the Sun

The sun is the great provider of life. It is a powerful healer and giver of warmth. Most food enjoys its days basking in the sun, growing sweet and ripe and nutrient rich. The sun blesses us with both light and warmth, two very powerful forms of energy. Drying foods helps concentrate even more of this powerful manna. By drying food, we get to concentrate even more sunlight into an already sun-laden food and thereby enhance the food with more energy.

Dried Foods for Travel

Dried foods have always been the choice for travelers. In ancient times, people would dry part of their harvest for winter or for a long migration to warmer climates. Even today, people going to work or school will bring dried fruit or nuts because they are lightweight and stable. Dried foods can be kept for considerably longer than when in fresh form. Dried foods are great for hiking because of the concentrated nutrition and energy. Dried foods are often dehydrating on the body, so be certain to drink lots of fluids or eat fresh foods to rehydrate the body.

Depicted below is a commercially purchased home dehydrator. These can be obtained through Loving Foods or your local health retailer.

How to Build Your Own Dehydrator

SOLAR

Step 1. Find a suitable cardboard or wooden box.

Step 2. Punch holes in the sides and bottom.

Step 3. Cover sides and bottom with dark-colored breathable screen or black cloth.

Step 4. Place a rack or hang a piece of breathable screen in the middle of the box.

Step 5. Put items to be dried on suspended screen.

Step 6. Cover box with glass or plastic.

Step 7. Place box in the sun.

Solar dehydration can be tricky. In some climates, the sun is too hot and it is best to use early morning sun. Other climates require all day drying. Be conscious of what you are drying the first few times to get an accurate gauge on how your climate affects the drying time. A plastic strip thermometer can be purchased at a tropical fish or pet store to give you an accurate temperature in the box.

ELECTRIC

Step 1. Find a suitable box. A cardboard box will work, yet for extended durability use a wooden box. Either build it yourself or use an old wooden trunk. Some people even turn an entire closet into a dehydrator. Ventilation is important, so make sure the moist evaporated air has some exit point.

Step 2. Purchase a small space heater, ideally with a built-in fan, and set it in the back of the box. You will probably need to cut a hole for the cord, the temperature setting, and on/off switch.

Step 3. Glue or nail thin slats of wood or cardboard to the side of the box in order to slide trays in and out.

Step 4. Create trays by making square frames of wood and covering them with a mesh or by taking cardboard squares, cutting out the centers, and lining them with screen.

Step 5. Put items to be dried on trays and turn on space heater.

A plastic strip thermometer can be purchased at a tropical fish or pet store to give you an accurate temperature in the box. If drying in your closet, you may want to take temperature readings at a variety of heights to find the most suitable drying area.

DRYING METHODS, TIME, AND TEMPERATURE

Food	Method	Drying Time	Temperature
Apple	Sliced	13 hours	108°F
Apple	Ground	10 hours	108°F
Banana	Whole	28 hours	108°F
Banana	Sliced	18 hours	108°F
Banana	Ground	14 hours	108°F
Carrot	Ground	8 hours	108°F
Coconut	Sliced	18 hours	108°F
Coconut	Ground	21 hours	108°F
Corn	Whole	18 hours	108°F
Corn	Ground	15 hours	108°F
Corn	Ground sprouts	15 hours	108°F
Flowers	Whole	3 to 5 hours	98°F
Garlic	Whole	12 hours	108°F
Garlic	Ground	8 hours	108°F
Herbs	Whole	5 to 7 hours	100°F
Kiwi	Sliced	16 hours	108°F
Mango	Sliced	21 hours	108°F
Melon	Sliced	24 hours	108°F
Melon	Ground	21 hours	108°F
Oat sprouts	Whole	15 hours	108°F

Food	Method	Drying Time	Temperature
Oat sprouts	Ground	24 hours	108°F
Onion	Sliced	13 hours	108°F
Onion	Ground	10 hours	108°F
Papaya	Sliced	20 hours	108°F
Papaya	Ground	16 hours	108°F
Peach	Sliced	24 hours	108°F
Peach	Ground	18 hours	108°F
Pear	Sliced	15 hours	108°F
Pear	Ground	13 hours	108°F
Persimmon	Whole	48 hours	108°F
Persimmon	Sliced	18 hours	108°F
Persimmon	Ground	15 hours	108°F
Pineapple	Sliced	21 hours	108°F
Potatoes	Sliced	16 hours	108°F
Sapodilla	Sliced	12 hours	108°F
Sea veggies	Whole	15 hours	100°F
Sprouts	Whole	13 hours	100°F
Sprouts	Ground	20 hours	100°F
Starfruit	Sliced	13 hours	108°F
Sunchoke	Sliced	16 hours	108°F
Tomato	Sliced	18 hours	108°F

Tips for the Foraging Raw Fooder

Where to Get Raw in a Cooked City

In most urban environments, there are farmers' markets where local growers come to sell their crops. Newspapers often provide good leads; otherwise, contact the local agricultural bureau or department of commerce for guidance. Metropolitan areas usually have a large number of health food stores to serve the different neighborhoods, along with organic or health-conscious restaurants that serve some raw foods on their menu. Check out the Yellow Pages™ under "health food" or buy a copy of *The Tofu Tollbooth* compiled by Dar Williams, which lists just about all the health-friendly places in the United States, state by state. One can find a wide range of exotic produce in ethnic neighborhoods in most major cities.

How to Forage in the Woods

Many wonderful plants found in the woods can be consumed. Almost every grass is edible, and some are very nutritious. The needles of the pine tree are edible; birch bark is edible; dandelion greens and flowers are edible. Most large fruits are edible. Many salad greens are available wild. It is a good idea to check out an herb and wild food guide for pictures of what each herb or green looks like. It is helpful to contact native or indigenous people to find more information about the edible plants in your area. Research is a valuable tool, so you can be prepared when a life-giving plant comes into season.

Foraging around Town

Many people live in houses with fruiting trees planted in their yard. Amazingly, people often prefer to buy from a store rather than pick for themselves. If you see fruit falling on the ground, consider knocking on the door or leaving a note asking whether it's okay to pick some of it. Many people will let you have all their fruit or will split the harvest with you.

Is It Really Organic?

In the money-making era we live in, one should be aware of what could be misrepresented on food labels. Often, produce that is grown locally may be organic even though it isn't stated. Organically grown means that the grower paid for the certification. All wild food is organic unless it was grown near heavily sprayed areas, and it is usually not certified. Some certified organic farms use natural rather than chemical fertilizers used in commercial farms, so use your best judgment in looking at the produce. If it is vibrant and you feel it might be organic, there is a good chance it is. Do what is right for your body. It is better to eat what your body needs than deprive yourself because of a label.

Raw Travel Tips

Finding Food

When adventuring to new places, it can be challenging to find raw organic food. One of the first places to look is in the Yellow Pages™ or on the Internet. In today's world, most businesses list themselves to make it easier for customers to find them. Look under health food, and also restaurants-vegetarian, and even sometimes under farms/fruit stands/farmers' markets. Once you find the healthy stores, take a look at their bulletin boards and pick up any health or new age magazines they may have for free. These places often have listings of everything from "fruit for sale" to "raw gatherings" and also may list restaurants. If all else fails, most supermarkets now have organic sections, so find the biggest one you can and make do with their commercially grown "organic" produce.

Airplanes

For airplane travel, it is best to bring your own food. This is the only way to ensure clean and fresh raw food. I've been told that a few airlines offer a raw option, and one airline offers only organic produce. These days it's challenging to get airline security to let you through without irradiating your food. If you happen to have food in your pockets, you can get a few things onboard without being irradiated. Otherwise, every bag and even your water go through the X-ray machine. The amount of radiation from the X-ray machines is supposedly less than that of a cell phone . . . yet this may just be safety propaganda. Personally, I either fast or bring what I can.

One of the best travel foods is kim chee. When they break out the cart of microwaved beef, open up your kim chee. It will mask the smell of airplane food and help build up good flora that airline radiation destroys.

Trains and Buses

On train and bus rides, it is easy to bring your own food. Certain whole foods travel better than others—watch out for squishages. Prepared foods are great for this kind of travel as well. Watermelon is one of my favorite travel foods. I just slice off the top and slowly eat across the inside avoiding the seeds.

Long Car Travel

Car travel gives you the best options of all. You can bring prepared food for parts of the road trip and collect many fruits along the way. Each new destination becomes a new source of food and fun. Sprouts can also be grown inside cars or buses by hanging sprout bags from the windows. Some people have even created solar dehydrators in the back window of their car.

Hotels

Hotels are great for preparing food and growing sprouts. You can set up a mini-kitchen area with a cutting board and even set up a blender. The bathroom can be used as a sprouting area, and you can stock up the room with local produce.

Raw Survival Foods

A few foods that are eaten raw can sustain the human body and give maximum energy for minimal consumption. These foods are power packed with concentrated nutrition and provide an abundance of vital energy. Diversity is important when eating raw, so it is challenging to live solely on these foods, yet it could be done if you were in a survival situation. Otherwise, these foods of sustenance are some great staples for a raw/living food way of eating.

Sprouted buckwheat: Buckwheat is the highest source of protein in the seed kingdom. Buckwheat is the fruit of a small herb plant and is praised as a staple in many Eastern countries. Buckwheat is easy to digest and is a wild food.

Chia seeds: Chia was one of the foods used by the Aztecs for hiking long distances. The chia seed, like flax, produces a saccharide gel around it that is an easily assimilatable starch. Chia is a power food.

Coconut water: This pure tree-filtered water is nearly identical to human blood plasma and has been used as a way to get intravenous medicine into the body instead of the IV liquid used in hospitals. Plasma makes up more than 55 percent of our blood content. Coconuts are more hydrating than water and more nutrient balanced for the human body.

Kelp: Seaweeds are the highest source of organic minerals available. Kelp is an excellent salt replacement and a great seasoning as well as a nutritional supplement. Kelp has more iron, magnesium, and trace minerals than any other substance known.

Spirulina: This single-celled alga is the sister plant to wheatgrass, providing a similar range of nutrients (all that are needed for survival), and spirulina is the highest source of protein on the planet (a whopping 89 percent). Spirulina has been used by the Aztecs as well for endurance.

Wheatgrass: The young shoots of the wheat plant are a great source of energy and nutrition. Wheatgrass is a power food and provides every vitamin and mineral necessary for human survival as well as helping to reduce radiation poisoning and remove other toxins from the body. Wheatgrass is protein packed, and one ounce of wheatgrass is equal nutritionally to four and a half pounds of vegetables.

Honey: The collected nectar of flowers is a potent and sustaining food. Honey gathered in the area you happen to be in grants a powerful immune booster and protects you from allergies. Honey is an ancient food and the honeybee, like the coconut, hasn't changed in over 20 million years. Honey comes from flowers and is gathered by bees in a completely natural and harmonious way. Just as the fruit that is sold in stores is gathered by workers, honey is collected by bees.

Raw Warnings

These warnings are designed to educate. We all make the best choices we can in each situation, and we grow as we go. Be patient, take your time, and vibrant health will follow behind.

Braggs Amino Acids: This product made only out of soybeans is still one of the most controversial "living food" products. At this point, no one knows how it is made. We do know that Paul Braggs was a health pioneer and that the other Braggs products are raw and living. There have been many questions about this product, and the answer is we still don't know. Braggs is non-GMO and supposedly "organic."

Nama shoyu: This is a fermented product made from soybeans, wheat, salt, and a starter. This product is cooked before being allowed to culture. This is a living food product as long as it is unpasteurized. The *Asperigillus oryzae* culture has proliferated so much by the time you purchase it that there are more culture and very few remnants of the soy-wheat soup that the culture lived in.

Nutritional yeast: This bacteria is superabundant in B vitamins, especially B-12 (one often lacking in a vegetarian diet). Some companies freeze-dry their yeast, while most kiln-dry it at 375°F for three seconds. It is essentially cooked, yet there are a few companies that still do it the old freezer way. Also, there are some companies that add things to their yeast. They are always listed, so just read the label.

Spirulina: Most spirulina is freeze-dried. This breaks open the cell wall (due to water expansion), increases the digestibility, and makes spirulina more absorbable. This freeze-drying process does destroy the life force (the ability to grow and create more life). A few companies still solar-dry their algae. Freeze-drying is considered raw by most, and so is spirulina.

Nori: Most nori contains fish! In fact, nori can be up to 10 percent fish and remain labeled as only nori. When nori is harvested, it is caught as a big mass of sea lettuce in nets. This wet seaweed is then lightly rinsed, put in a big blender, and then spread out like paper to dry. A few companies provide a fish-free nori (Buddhist and kosher varieties).

Sea vegetables (hijiki, arame, and so on): Most of the sea vegetables sold in packages have been cooked. It says on the back of packages of arame and hijiki that they are cooked for several hours before sun drying. Just because it says sun dried doesn't mean it wasn't cooked first.

Nuts and nut butters: There is a huge question about how nuts and seeds are dried. Many seeds such as sesame are hulled using steam. Some places still machine hull. Nuts must be dried before selling, and many companies dry in kilns and ovens at well over 200°F. Nut butters that are made from "raw" nuts are sold as raw even if the nut butter–making equipment heated up to well over 200°F. Truly raw nuts are usually freeze-dried.

Young Thai coconuts: These raw coconuts imported fresh from Thailand are definitely *not* organic. These nuts have been treated with various chemicals, including formaldehyde and bleach, and are processed by machines.

Sea salt /Celtic sea salt: Watch out for iodized salts and kiln-dried mineral salts. Sun-dried salt is the best.

Apples and cucumbers: For the purpose of shelf life and aesthetic visual beauty, apples and cucumbers are often waxed with a synthetic or carnuba wax. These items are labeled organic and have been grown organically. Later, they are treated by the shipping or distribution company.

Anything organically grown: Organic doesn't mean consciously grown. Many organic farms are using conventional methods that are harmful to the environment and are farming for money rather than to produce good healthy natural food. Biodynamically grown foods are more conscious, yet only foods you get from farmers or grow yourself are truly consciously grown and sustainable. It is important to be able to eat locally year-round or store up local supplies in summer and fall for winter, because any food that must be transported by planes, trains, boats, trucks, and cars is not truly sustainable. The food comes from far away, and it has been said that 70 percent of the world's transportation is used for moving food. That is a lot of fuel and wasted time. Think globally. Eat locally.

Honey: Many beekeepers harm the bees when they collect the honey. Some smoke out the bees, or even fumigate the hive. Many commercial hives have all the honey removed and leave none for the bees during the winter. Tropical honey is usually the safest bet since there are always flowers and therefore always more honey nectar to collect. Some honey contains larvae (baby bees) and this is not vegan. Many beekeepers use separators to keep the queen out of the top layers so the eggs don't get laid in that honey. Be sure to get honey from a source you trust, and make sure they are using non-impregnated cells to claim their golden nectar.

Cacao: Cacao beans, or nibs, are becoming ever popular in the raw food scene. While cacao may have some helpful properties, such as amino acid compositions and high levels of antioxidants, it can also be toxic and cause mild hallucinations at dosages over 40 beans. Cacao is shunned by all animals in nature and domesticated animals that are fed cacao often contract cancer and can die of toxicity. Cacao contains a chemical very similar to caffeine that acts a stimulant on the central nervous system, causing extreme mood swings and aggressive tendencies.

Agave nectar: The nectar from the agave cactus is used by many people in the living food world as a sweetener. When harvested fresh, this sweet liquid is similar to maple water or coconut water. In order to stabilize it and concentrate the sugars, agave is heated to temperatures above 150°. This prevents it from fermenting and turning into alcohol. Commercially-available agave nectar is a cooked product. It can, however, be obtained in its pure, raw form.

Easy Indoor Gardening

Many plants grow easily indoors. Indoor gardening can be crucial for city survival or just to supplement your winter diet with fresh home-grown foods. Sprouts are the most nutritious and most rapidly growing of any indoor-grown food. Please refer to the section on sprouting in this book for further information. Beet tops can grow beet greens, and celery bottoms will grow leaves. Beets and other greens can easily be grown by placing the top of the beet or the bottom of the celery stalk in a shallow tray or dish of water. After a few days, the greens begin to grow and can be harvested for many weeks. Herbs grow indoors year-round, especially basil and parsley. Just provide a bit of light and nourishing soil plus an ample dosage of water and you will have a beautiful array of indoor-grown herbs. Even hot pepper plants and edible flowers can be easily grown indoors year-round. Indoor growing systems are also a good way to grow vegetable and bushy fruit crops as well as an abundant supply of herbs. Hydroponic (water-grown) or just traditional soil-grown plants can be grown indoors. This may require supplemental lighting (fluorescent, halide, sodium) in order to get a substantial crop. There are many books and guides to growing everything from tomatoes to strawberries in a basement or warehouse. Greenhouses and solariums are some of the best ways to grow your own food year-round.

Types of Raw Food Diets

Raw foods: This is a general term referring to those who consume a diet of foods prepared without any fire. A person following the raw foods diet may not be vegan, but is likely to be vegetarian. Raw foodists often attempt to properly combine their foods.

Live foods: People eating a live food diet eat all raw foods (often with the exception of nightshades) as well as live foods. Live foods may be cooked and then have a living culture introduced to them. This culture will then grow upon the cooked food, and as it breaks down it creates more cultures. Some examples are miso, tofu, and amazake. Live foods are not necessarily cooked. Some raw/live examples are rejuvelac, sprouts, and seed cheez.

Living foods: A living foods diet is a synthesis of raw foods and living foods. The teachings of living foods have been expounded by Dr. Ann Wigmore. Living food eaters will eat all raw foods as well as raw living. Living foodists often include wheatgrass as a major part of their diet as well as a range of cultured foods.

Essenes: The Essenes were a sect that lived over 2,000 years ago. They sun dried their breads and sprouted their seeds. A large portion of their diet was made up of fruits. The Essenes also understood much about intentional eating and bodily cleansing for healing.

Breatharians: A breatharian is someone who consumes no food or drink. People following this path are very few because of the extreme nature of the discipline required. Most breatharians reside in areas where they do not have to interact with society. The few I know do not have jobs or cars or even go to towns. Many breatharians will sit and meditate with a piece of fruit in order to "absorb its essence"; other say they exist on prana, "air/energy."

Fruitarians: Fruitarians are those who ingest only fruit. Some fruitarians eat only one type of fruit at a time, while others will eat any fruit in any combination. This type of diet is better suited to those who live in warmer climates.

Sproutarians: People who consume only sprouts are known as sproutarians. Sprouts are the youngest stage of growth for a plant. They have the highest vitality and nutritional value at three to seven days' growth. There are two types of sprouts, hydroponic and soil based. Some young grasses are considered sprouts.

Hydrorians: Hydrorians, or liquidarians, are people who ingest foods only in a liquid form. Fresh juices make up the primary diet of these people. Some hydrorians do not drink water, while others make it a primary part of their diet.

Natural hygiene: Natural hygiene (NH) is a type of raw diet that involves the use of only completely natural substances. Natural hygienists do not use shampoo, soap, cleansers, or other "beauty products." The rest of the diet is varied. Many of the different NH groups disagree about general principles. NH is based upon the teachings of H. Shelton, T. C. Fry, and Viktoria Bidwell.

Instincto: This diet is all raw. The instinctos eat anything raw: plants, animals, insects, and so forth. They believe in eating one type of thing at a time (for example, only mangos or only spiders). Instinctos eat based on instinct, as the name suggests.

Vitarian: The vitarian diet is based on the teachings of Dr. Johnny Lovewisdom. Essentially, this is a raw, mostly fruit-based diet. One primary practice is the retention of sexual fluids in order to extend life.

Sun foods: Sun foods are foods that are blessed by the sun. This includes mostly fresh foods. The sun food system uses a food pyramid that balances sweet foods, fatty foods, and green foods to keep the body in its ideal state.

Life food nutrition: Life food nutrition is the use of food as medicine. This is a branch of raw food that is conscious of the glycolytic rate of foods (how their sugars are processed in the body and specifically how they affect the liver). Life foodists choose to not eat any starchy foods, such as carrots or bananas. Essential oils, such as flax or hemp, are an important part of this diet. Life food is also very big on nutritional fasting, which is fasting on blended foods. Life food is a part of whole brain functioning, which also includes other physical and psychological tools to aid in healing.

Loving foods: The philosophy of loving foods is that at every intention, from planting seeds to the point of ingestion, food affects us. Loving foods advocates the use of all vegan raw-living organic foods. The theory is that every hand, machine, and tool that touches our foods adds to the intention being put into the food. Anyone who has eaten food made by an angry chef knows the difference between that and food made by someone you love. Foods prepared with proper intention will nourish the body far more than foods that go through a range of harsh experiences and then sit in a supermarket only to be microwaved and eaten. Loving foods believes in acquiring foods as close to the source as possible. Grow your own or buy from your local farmer and always grow sprouts. A loving foods diet does not include any animals or animal-based products (eggs, dairy), heavily refined products (sugar, flour), or pesticides and chemicals. Loving foods advocates the use of the four living food groups to create a balanced raw food diet. Loving foods also sees the value of exercise and right livelihood to create true balance, health, and happiness.

Raw Friendly Restaurants

Alaska

Enzyme Express
1330 East Huffman Road
Anchorage, AK 99515
(907) 345-1330

Jen's Restaurant
Olympic Center
701 West 36th Avenue
Anchorage, AK 99503
(907) 561-5367
jens@alaska.net
www.jensrestaurant.com

Arizona

Anjali-Botanica
330 East Seventh Street
Tucson, AZ 85705
(520) 623-0913
info@anjali.com
www.anjali.com

Rawsome Café
(at Gentle Strength Co-op)
Tempe, AZ 85281
(480) 496-5959
info@rawforlife.com
www.rawforlife.com

Tree of Life
771 Harshaw Road
Patagonia, AZ 85624
(520) 394-2589
www.treeoflife.nu

California

The 418 Organic Café
418 Front Street
Santa Cruz, CA 95060
(831) 425-LIVE

Au Lac Vegetarian Cafe
16563 Brookhurst Street
Fountain Valley, CA 92708
(714) 418-0658
www.aulac.com

Back to the Garden
21065 Bush Street
Middletown, CA 95461
(707) 987-8303
Julia@sacreddance.org
www.sacreddance.org

Beverly Hills Juice Club
8382 Beverly Boulevard
Beverly Hills, CA 90048
(323) 655-8300

Castle Rock Inn
5827 Sacramento Avenue
Dunsmuir, CA 96025
(530) 235-0782
bill@castlerockpub.com
www.castlerockpub.com

Cilantro Live!
315-1/2 Third Avenue
Chula Vista, CA 91910
(619) 827-7401, (619) 827-7403
www.cilantrolive.com

Eatopia
5001 Newport Avenue
Ocean Beach, CA 92107
(619) 224-3237
eatopia@eatopiaexpress.com
www.eatopiaexpress.com

Good Mood Food Deli Café
5930 Warner Avenue
Huntington Beach, CA 92646
(714) 377-2028

Gratitude
400 Harrison Street
San Francisco, CA 94105
(415) 824-4652

Harvest and Rowe
55 Second Street
San Francisco, CA 94105
(415) 541-7771
www.harvestandrowe.com

Inn of the Seventh Ray
128 Old Topanga Canyon Road
Topanga, CA 90290
(310) 455-1311

Millennium Restaurant
246 McAllister Street
San Francisco, CA 94102
(415) 487-9800

Napoleon
2301 Main Street
Santa Monica, CA 90401
(310) 721-4222

Raw Energy Café
2050 Addison Street
Berkeley, CA 94702
(510) 665-9464
info@rawenergy.net
www.rawenergy.net

Colorado

Turtle Lake Refuge
826 East Third Avenue
Durango, CO 81301
(970) 247-8395

District of Columbia

Delights of the Garden
2616 Georgia Avenue N.W.
Washington, DC 20001
(202) 319-8747

Source of Life Juice Bar
Everlasting Life Health Food Supermarket
2928 Georgia Avenue N.W.
Washington, DC 20001
(202) 232-1700
www.everlastinglife.net

Florida

Dining in the Raw
800 Olivia Street
Key West, FL 33040
(305) 295-2600

Food Without Fire
419B Española Way
Miami Beach, FL 33139
(305) 674-9960

Living Greens
205 McLeod Street
Merritt Island, FL 32953
(321) 454-2268
www.living-greens.com

Suzanne's Vegi Bistro
7251 Biscayne Boulevard
Miami, FL 33138
(305) 758-5859

Georgia

Life Grocery & Cafe
1453 Roswell Road
Marietta, GA 30062
(770) 977-9583
www.lifegrocery.com

Living Foods Institute
1530 Dekalb Avenue N.E., Suite E
Atlanta, GA 30307
(404) 524-4488
(800) 844-9876
info@livingfoodsinstitute.com

Lush Life Cafe
1405 Ralph D. Abernathy
Boulevard
Atlanta, GA 30303
(404) 758-8737

Raw
878 Ralph D. Abernathy Boulevard
Atlanta, GA 30303
(404) 758-1110

Sprout Café
1475 Holcolm Bridge Road,
Suite 200
Roswell, GA 30076
(770) 992-9218
www.sproutcafe.com

Hawaii

Joy's Place
1993 South Kihei Road
Kihei, Maui, HI 96779
(808) 879-9258

Raw Experience
P.O. Box 790358
Paia, Maui, HI 96779
(310) 729-3663
Private dining

Idaho

Akasha Organics
160 North Main Street
Ketchum, ID 83340
(208) 726-4777, (208) 726-0081
akasha@svidaho.net

Illinois

Karyn's
1901 North Halsted Avenue
Chicago, IL 60614
(312) 255-1590
karynraw@aol.com
www.karynraw.com

Massachusetts

Basil Chef Cuisine
13-R Bessom Street
Marblehead, MA 01945
(781) 864-9250
sue@basilchef.com

Organic Garden Restaurant
and Juice Bar
294 Cabot Street
Beverly, MA 01915
(978) 922-0004

Minnesota

Ecopolitan
2409 Lyndale Avenue S.
Minneapolis, MN 55405
(612) 874-7336
info@ecopolitan.net
www.ecopolitan.net

Nevada

The Raw Truth
3620 East Flamingo Road
Las Vegas, NV 89212
(702) 450-9007

New Jersey

Down to Earth
7 Broad Street
Red Bank, NJ 07701
(732) 747-4542

New Mexico

Green Life Organic
105B Quensnel Street
Taos, NM 87571
(505) 751-4212

New York

Bonobo's Vegetarian
18 East 23rd Street
New York, NY 10010
(212) 505-1200
eatraw1@aol.com
www.bonobosrestaurant.com

Caravan of Dreams
405 East Sixth Street
New York, NY 10009
(212) 254-1613

Eatraw
426 15th Street and 8th Avenue
Brooklyn, NY 11215
atillman@eatraw.com
www.eatraw.com

Green Paradise
609 Vanderbilt Avenue
Brooklyn, NY 11201
(718) 230-5177
ckrmr@cs.com

Integral Yoga
227 West 13th Street
New York, NY 10011
(212) 929-0586
Raw foods at deli.

Jubbs Longevity Center
508 East 12th Street
New York, NY 10009
Contact: Narda
(212) 353-5000
narda@lifefood.com
www.jubbslongevity.com

Lifetyme Grocery
410 Sixth Avenue
New York, NY 10011
(212) 420-9099
Life food at the deli counter.

Quintessence
263 East 10th Street
New York City, NY 10009
(646) 654-1823
quintessence-rest@worldnet.att.net
www.quintessencerestaurant.com

Quintessence
566 Amsterdam Avenue
New York, NY 10024

Quintessence
353 East 78th Street
New York, NY 10021

Spirit
530 West 27th
New York, NY 10001

Think Liquid Juice Bar
1489 First Avenue
New York, NY 10022
(212) 327-2703, (212) 628-1319
www.thinkliquid.com

Oregon

Well Springs Garden Cafe
2253 Highway 99
Ashland, OR 97520
(541) 488-6486

Pennsylvania

Arnold's Way
319 West Main Street
Store #4 Rear
Lansdale, PA 19446
(215) 361-0116
www.arnoldsway.com

Oasis Living Cuisine
Great Valley Center
Malvern, PA 19355
(610) 647-9797
info@oasislivingcuisine.com
www.oasislivingcuisine.com

Texas

Pure
2720 Greenville Avenue
Dallas, TX 75206
Contact: Cynthia Beavers
(214) 824-7776
rawfoodchef@aol.com
www.purerawcafe.com

Raw Truth Cafe
3815 Live Oak
Houston, TX 77004-4529
(713) 523-9755

Washington

Choco Canyon
50th and 12th by University
Seattle, WA 98101

Canada

Les Vivres
4434 Street Dominique
Montréal, Québec H2X 2X1
(514) 842-3479

Live Health Café
258 Dupont Street
Toronto, Ontario M5R 1V7
(416) 515-2002

Raw
1849 West First Avenue
Vancouver, BC V6J 538
(604) 737-0420, (604) 737-0430

Super Sprouts
720 Bathurst Street
Toronto, Ontario M5S 2R4
(416) 977-7796

International

Earl's Juice Garden
16 Derrymore Road
Kingston 10
Jamaica
(876) 906-4287

Heartstone
Parkway, Camden Town
London NW1 7PN
England

Restaurant Hiltl
Sihlstrasse 28
Zurich ZH 8001
Switzerland
+41 1 277 70 00

Saru Dori
The Fresh Food Kitchen at Ubud
Sari Health Resort
35 Jalan Kajeng
Ubud, Bali 80571
Indonesia
62 361 974 393

Vita Organic
279c Finchley Road
London NW3 6ND
England
020 74 35 21 88
www.vitaorganic.com

Healing and Educational Centers

USA

California

East County Holistic Care
3168 Florine Drive
Lemon Grove, CA 91945
(619) 589-7546

Eden Retreats
Nature's First Law
San Diego, CA 92190
(888) 729-3663
nature@rawfood.com
www.rawfood.com

The Fire Within, Inc.
4 Admiral Drive, #424
Emeryville, CA 94608
(510) 653-5050
jon@thefirewithin.com
www.thefirewithin.com

Living Light Culinary
Arts Institute
704 North Harrison
Fort Bragg, CA 95437
(800) 816-2319, (707) 964-2420
info@rawfoodchef.com
www.rawfoodchef.com

Malibu Phoenix Retreat Center
Escondido Phoenix Ranch
Malibu, CA 90263
malibuphoenix@charter.net
www.malibuphoenix.com

Optimum Health Institute (OHI)
6970 Central Avenue
Lemon Grove, CA 91945
(619) 464-3346, (619) 589-4098

Florida

Hippocrates Health Institute
1443 Palmdale Court
West Palm Beach, FL 33411
(800) 842-2125, (561) 471-9464

Georgia

The Living Foods Institute
1530 Dekalb Avenue N.E., Suite E
Atlanta, GA 30307
(404) 524-4488

Shinui Living Foods Institute
1085 Lake Charles Drive
Roswell, GA 30075
(770) 992-9218
www.shinuiretreat.com

Hawaii

Gentle World
P.O. Box 238
Kapa'au, Big Island, HI 96755
gentle@aloha.net
www.gentleworld.com

Hono Hu´Aka Tropical Plantation
P.O. Box 600
Haiku, Maui, HI 96708
(808) 573-1391, (808) 573-0141
info@retreatmaui.com
www.retreatmaui.com

Loving Foods Institute
P.O. Box 790358
Paia, Maui, HI 96779
(310) 729-3663
allraw@lovingfoods.com
www.lovingfoods.com

Pure Kauai
Kauai, HI
(866) 457-7873
info@purekauai.com
www.purekauai.com

Yoga Oasis
P.O. Box 1935
Pahoa, Big Island, HI 96778
(800) 274-4446
info@yogaoasis.org
www.yogaoasis.org

Michigan

Assembly of Yahweh
Wellness Center
7881 Columbia Highway
Eaton Rapids, MI 48827
(517) 663-1637

Creative Health Institute
112 West Union City Road
Union City, MI 49094
(517) 278-6260, (517) 278-5837
creative@coldwater.net
www.creativehealthusa.com

New Mexico

Ann Wigmore Foundation
P.O. Box 399
San Fide, NM 87049
(505) 552-0595

New York

Alok Holistic Health Centre
224 East Seventh Street, Suite 13
New York, NY 10009
(212) 388-1516
info@alokhealth.com

Jubb's Longevity Lifefood Store and
Health Clinic
508 East 12th Street
New York, NY 10009
(888) 420-8270, (212) 358-8068
www.jubbslongevity.com

North Carolina

School of Natural Hygiene
326 Victory Lane
Shelby, NC 28152
(704) 480-9737
sniadach@connectu.net

Oregon

Wild Food Adventures
5036 Southeast Mitchell Street
Portland, OR 97206
(503) 775-3828

Texas

Dr. Cinque's Health Retreat
305 Verdin Drive
Buda, TX 78610
(512) 295--4256
drcinque@hotmail.com
www.drcinque.com

Optimum Health Institute (OHI)
Rural Route 1, Box 339-J
Cedar Creek, TX 98612
(512) 303-4817, (512) 303-1239

Rest of Your Life Health Retreat
P.O. Box 102
Barksdale, TX 78828
(830) 234-3488
vvvhaag@swtexas.net

Washington

The Annapurna Inn
538 Adams Street
Port Townsend, WA 98368
(899) 868-2662
annapurna@olympus.net
www.annapurnaretreat-spa.com

Canada

New Life Retreat
RR4 Dobbie Road
Lanark, Ontario KOG 1KO
(613) 259-3337, (613) 259-3103
healing@newliferetreat.com
www.newliferetreat.com

Nonpareil Natural Health Retreat
RR#3
Stirling, Ontario KOK 3EO
(613) 395 6332
nonpareil@sympatico.ca

Asia

Hippocrates Health Resort of Asia
The Farm at San Benito
119 Brangay Tipakan
Lipa City, Batangas
Philippines
1 800 927 25 27, ext 202
katharine.clark@thefarm.com.ph
www.thefarm.com.ph

Oiko and Melisande
Bukit Lawang
Sumatra, Indonesia
auxsources@yahoo.com

Rainbow Community
Thailand
raunetty@yahoo.com
www.come.to/apamada

Ubud Sari Health Resort
35 Jalan Kajeng
Ubud, Bali 80571
Indonesia
62 361 97 43 93, 62 361 97 63 05
www.ubudsari.com

Australia

Clohesy River Health Farm
P.O. Box 901
Cairns, QLD 4870
07 4053 77 86, 07 4051 01 77
academy.natural.living@iig.
com.au
www.iig.com.au/anl

Hippocrates Health Centre of
Australia
Elaine Avenue, Mudgeeraba
Gold Coast, QLD 4213
07 5530 28 60
www.hippocrates.com.au

Unwinding Retreat
Bulby Close
Dyers Crossing, NSW 2429
02 6550 23 40
unwindingretreat@tsn.cc

Britain

Detox Your World Retreats
Shazzie
Cambridgeshire
44 8700 113 119, 44 8700 114 119
info@detoxyourworld.com
www.detoxyourworld.com

Eart4: London Healing Arts &
Living Nutrition Centre
Effat
020 88 41 14 36
living3@email.com

Harmonious Living
www.harmonious-living.com

Heartspring Raw Guest House
Hill House
Llansteffan Carmarthen
South Wales SA33 5JG
01267 241 999
info@heartspring.co.uk
www.heartspring.co.uk

Karuna Retreats
Dao and Shoshana
info@karunaretreats.com
www.home-colonics.com

True Health Healing Centre
22 Webber Close
Ogwell, Devon TQ12 6YL
1626 352 765
www.vibrancy.homestead.com/
pageone.html

The UK Centre For Living Foods
Elaine Bruce
Holmleigh, Gravel Hill
Ludlow SY8 1QS
44 845 330 45 07, 44 845 330 45 08
elaine@livingfoods.co.uk
www.livingfoods.co.uk

Caribbean

Ann Wigmore Institute
P.O. Box 429
Rincón, Puerto Rico 00677
(787) 868-6307, (787) 868-2430
wigmore@coqui.net
www.annwigmore.org

Cascada Verde
Apdo 888
8000 San Isidro P.Z.
Costa Rica
cascadaverde@hotmail.com
www.cascadaverde.org

Otas Holistic Health Center
461 Circular Drive Lange Park
Chaguanas, Trinidad
1 868 665 36 35
sat@carib-link.net

Finland

The Institute of Living Food
22930 Fiskö
Aland, Finland
358 18 56285
fisko@aland.net
www.co.jyu.fi/finlandweb/institute/brochure.htm

France

Albert Mosséri
25 Rue du Grand Pré
10290 Rigny-la-Nonneuse

Mexico

Sanoviv Medical Institute
800 726 68 48
www.sanoviv.com

Portugal

Casa Nirvana
Moncarapacho, Algarve, 8700
351 289 79 20 93
sales@holistichealth.co.uk
www.holistichealth.co.uk

South Africa

High Rustenberg Hydro
Idas Valley, Rustenberg Road
Stellenbosch 7600 Western Cape
27 21 883 86 00, 27 21 886 51 63
reservations@thehydro.co.za
www.thehydro.co.za

The Natural Hygiene Clinic
Dr. D. Karalis
39 Talbragar Avenue
Craighall 2196
Johannesburg
27 11 880 43 37, 27 11 447 86 66
dr.karalis@global.co.za
www.home.global.co.za/-dkaralis/

Spain

Ecoforest
Apdo. Correos 29
29100 Coín
Málaga
34 661 07 99 50
info@ecoforest.org
www.ecoforest.org

Hara And Carlo Davies
Lista de Correos
Icod de los Vinos
38439 Tenerife
Canary Islands
34 676 43 89 36

Societies and Support Groups

This section lists groups that meet to discuss topics related to raw and living foods, present living food lectures, and have raw food potlucks. Please contact them because meeting places do change. The addresses and phone numbers listed are for the people coordinating the groups and are not necessarily where the groups meet.

Alaska

Dr. Andrea Iverson, DC
(907) 463-5557

Arizona

Living Community Center
330 East Seventh Street
Tucson, AZ 85705
(520) 623-0913
Jason@livingcommunitycenter.com
www.livingcommunitycenter.com

Raw Foods Network of Tucson
124 North Norris Avenue
Tucson AZ 85719
(520) 792-9283

Raw for Life
Phoenix, AZ
(480) 496-5959
Charles Thomas Mort and Tanya Ferguson
info@rawforlife.com
www.rawforlife.com

Sedona/Verde Valley
Raw Foods Community Gathering
Cottonwood, AZ 86326
(928) 649-3451
verdevalleyraw@yahoo.com

Tree of Life Rejuvenation Center
P.O. Box 778
Patagonia, AZ 85624
(520) 394-2520
healing@treeoflife.nu
www.treeoflife.nu

Arkansas

L.O.V.E.-I.N.G.
(Longevity from Organic Vegetarian Enzymatic Indigenous-Indoor Nutriceutical Garden)
P.O. Box 1556
Mt. Ida, AR 71957
(870) 867-4521
youthing@alltel.net
www.naturalusa.com/viktor/sanctuary.html

Raw Ozarks
info@rawozarks.com
www.rawozarks.com

California

East Bay Living Foods
1300 Grand Street
Alameda, CA 94501
www.living-foods.com/eastbay

East Bay Living Foods Group
(415) 789-8005
eastbaylivingfoods@yahoo.com

Essene Church Services and Potluck
San Francisco, CA 94117
(415) 885-2251

Greater Sacramento Living
Food Community
6130-A Madison Avenue
Carmichael, CA 95608
(916) 705-8921
gslfc@yahoo.com

Inland Empire Raw
Riverside, CA 92501
Kathleen
(909) 370-1271
rawgirl@msn.com

L.A. Area Potluck and Lecture
7860 Willoughby Avenue
Los Angeles, CA 90046
(323) 653-6314

L.A. Living Foods Community
http://health.groups.yahoo.com/
group/LosAngelesLivingFoods

Living Food Enthusiasts
3640 Garden Bar Road
Lincoln, CA 95648
(415) 751-2806 (sproutline)
sflife@living-foods.com

Living Light House
1457 12th Street
Santa Monica, CA 90401
(310) 395-6337
knicely@hotmail.com

Marin Living Foods Community
Aldersgate Methodist Church
1 Well Brock Heights
San Rafael, CA 94903
(415) 883-5201
vibrantlife4u@earthlink.net

Modesto Potlucks
518 Kimble Street
Modesto, CA 95350
(209) 571-8272
optimismone@aol.com

Monterey County Raw
Foods Network
Carmel Crossroads
Community Room
Anna Masteller
(408) 620-0520
foodinthenude@rawfoods.com

Jim Montrose and Zaida Rivene
2133 Pullman Avenue
Belmont, CA 94002
(650) 591-5125

Natural Hygiene Los Angeles
Sophie Holzgreen
(213) 388-4332

North Bay Living Foods Community
3000 Santa Rosa Avenue
Santa Rosa, CA 95401
(707) 793-2365
www.beraw.com

North Tahoe Raw Food Group
Kings Beach, CA
Christine Hale
(530) 386-0875

Orange County Raw
(949) 651-6309
simplyraw@ocraw.com

Raw Sacramento
www.rawsacramento.net

Raw Tawk Redondo Beach
Michele DeMarco
(310) 902-7027
miche517@adelphia.net

Sacramento Potlucks
Christian Blackburn
(916) 325-0500
webmaster@rawsacramento.org
www.rawsacramento.org

San Diego Raw Potluck Group
Chris and Melina O'Loughlin
(619) 204-4903
chris@rawtrainer.com
www.rawtrainer.com

San Luis Obispo Living Foods Group
Genie Sumrall
(805) 543-4405
healthEwoman@juno.com

San Mateo Rawfoods Group
Yoga Wellness Center
35 North San Mateo Drive
San Mateo, CA 94401
smrawfoodsgroup@yahoo.com

SDC Living Foods Support Group of San Diego County
Helene Idels
P.O. Box 3397
Vista, CA 92085
(619) 364-6968
nomad@rawfoods.com

SF Life
Dorleen Tong
San Francisco, CA
(415) 751-2806

South Bay Living Food Community
660 Hayne Road
Hillsbourgh, CA 94010
(650) 401-6423
info@vibrantliving.org

The Subud House
3800 Old San Jose Road
Soquel, CA 95073
(831) 458-9532
dhilyard@aol.com

Colorado

Boulder Potlucks
cgiambri@yahoo.com

Colorado Springs
curlychef@adelphia.net

Dining in the Raw
9397 West 45th Avenue
Wheat Ridge, CO 80033
(303) 467-0813
starwulf@prodigy.net

Delaware

Newark Support and Potlucks
Dhrumil Purohit
(302) 559-8082
dhrumil@dharmaboost.com
www.dharmaevents.com

District of Columbia

Vegetarian Society of D.C.
David Cohen
raw@vsdc.org
http://vsdc.org/raw.html

Florida

Fort Myers Live
Tim Palzer
livinggenesis129@aol.com

Miami Live!
Key Biscayne Congregational Church
355 Glenridge Road
Key Biscayne, FL 33149
Karen, (305) 672-5878
mmiamilive@gardenofhealth.com,
www.gardenofhealth.com/miamilive/

Ron Radstrom
Southern Botanicals
611 South Myrtle Avenue, Unit D
Clearwater, FL 33756
healthfree@healthfree.com

Sarasota Potlucks
Esse Hopper
goproraw@comcast.net

Georgia

Atlanta Live Vegan Potluck
1530 Dekalb Avenue N.E., Suite E
Atlanta, GA 30307
(404) 524-4488
info@lovingfoodsinstitute.com
www.livingfoodsinstitute.com

Marietta Sprout Raw Food Group
The Natural Market Place
Marietta, GA 30008
gideongraff@mindspring.com
www.sproutrawfood.org

Sprout of Life Cafe
1453 Roswell Road
Marietta, GA 30008
www.sproutcafe.com

Hawaii

Loving Foods Society
P.O. Box 790358
Paia, Maui, HI 96779
(310) 729-3663

Illinois

H.E.A.L. (Healthy Eating
Alternative Living)
Eva LaRoche
Oak Forest, IL 60452
(708) 535-1174

Saturday Night Live
Interfaith Center
913 South Illinois Avenue
Carbondale, IL 62901
(618) 351-6308
treesong@treesong.org
http://treesong.org/satur-
daynightlive

Indiana

Bloomington Potluck
Liz Overton
3740 East Third Street
Bloomington, IN 47401
(812) 332-3372

Louisiana

New Orleans Potluck
Fairgrounds Coffee House
Stephanie Mayoral
(504) 621-2596

Maryland

Baltimore Potluck
3443 Guilford Terrace
Baltimore, MD 21218
Margie Roswell
(410) 467-3727
mroswell@charm.net
http://rawbaltimore.com
www.rawfoodwiki.org

Live Food Support Group
of Maryland
5426 Beale Place
Churchton, MD 20733
(410) 832-5181

Tanglewood Wellness Center
6135 Mountaindale Road
Thurmont, MD 21788
(301) 898-8901
ingo@tanglewoodwellnesscenter.com
www.tanglewoodwellnesscenter.com

Massachusetts

Spring of Light
10 North Main Street
Avon, MA 02322
(877)-SURVIVE, (877)-RAWFOOD

Michigan

Lansing Raw Food Group
hihomin@comcast.net
www.livinghiho.com

Living Foods Support Michigan
210 West Lake Lansing Road
P.O. Box 25064
East Lansing, MI 48909
(517) 337-3912

Living Food Support Group
First Christian Church
1001 Chester Road
Lansing, MI 48906
(517) 882-1033
clott@voyager.net

Minnesota

Twin Cities Living Foods Community
1725 Grand Avenue
St. Paul, MN 55101
Nancy Hone
(651) 647-9908
cstoutland@nwchiro.edu

Missouri

Natural Hygiene Society
6127 Kingsbury Avenue
St. Louis, MO 63112
(314) 863-6321

Raw Foods Foundation
6333 North Rosebury, 1W
St. Louis, MO 63105
(314) 725-6085
(573) 598-9908
rawfoods@earthlink.net
gardencart@semo.net

Nevada

Las Vegas Raw!
www.groups.yahoo.com/group/lasvegasraw

New Jersey

New Jersey Raw Food Events
http://superbeingdiet.com/njevents.htm

New Mexico

Albuquerque Living Foods Community
(505) 898-9434
Will.Dodge@nmshtd.state.nm.us
www.cnsp.com/dodger/nmraw/raw.html

Santa Fe Living Foods Community
(505) 424-2258, (505) 737-3045
Will.Dodge@nmshtd.state.nm.us
www.cnsp.com/dodger/nmraw/raw.html

Taos Living Foods Community
(505) 758-1280
Will.Dodge@nmshtd.state.nm.us
www.cnsp.com/dodger/nmraw/raw.html

New York

Accent on Wellness
33 East Seventh Street
New York, NY 10003-8001
Donna Perrone
(212) 760-5953, (212) 722-7901
perroned@aol.com
www.live-food.com

Brooklyn Raw Food Potluck
Park Slope Food Co-op
782 Union Street
Brooklyn, NY 11215
webperson@live-food.com
www.live-food.com/braw.html

Brooklyn Raw Foods Support Group
Eco Books
192 Fifth Avenue
Park Slope, Brooklyn, NY 11217
Tom Paul
(718) 832-9380, (718) 499-6984
ramiller@interport.net

Buffalo and West NY Potluck
Sharon Krawczyk
(716) 892-7394
sharonsky@webtv.net
http://groups.yahoo.com/group.rawfoodistswny/join

Ithaca Raw Food Group
Bob and Beacon Orshalom
(607) 256-3315

Long Island Support Group
Rockville Centre Senior Center
Rockville Centre, NY 11570
(516) 431-7920, (516) 431-2508
sethdavis99@hotmail.com

Planet Health
319 East Ninth Street
New York, NY 10003
(212) 722-7901

Rhio's Raw Food Hotline
New York, NY 10013
(212) 343-1152

Rochester Potluck
12 Greyson Road
Rochester, NY 14623
(585) 279-0242
http://home.rochester.rr.com/sevenahm

Westchester Raw Food Support Group
Nancy Durand-Lanson
(914) 941-0042

North Carolina

Ashville Raw Living Food Family
Grace Shen
Ashville, NC 28804
Rawgirl2000@yahoo.com

Cary Potluck
(919) 319-6758

Greensboro Potluck
gardenharvest@yahoogroups.com

Hickory Potluck
1985 Tate Boulevard S.E.
Hickory, NC 28602
Pat Benfield
(828) 304-9096
pbenfield@braininjuryspecialists.com

Ohio

Hallelujah Health Seekers
Healthy for Him
2305 Front Street
Cuyahoga Falls, OH 44221
rwandling@neo.rr.com

Oregon

Essene Church and Potluck
Portland, OR
(541) 895-2190

Eugene Potlucks
Phyllis Linn
(541) 463-0800
raweugene@mindspring.com

Living Health Network
1538 Southeast 122nd Avenue, #49
Portland, OR 97233
(503) 256-8351
rawimmortal@hotmail.com

Portland Free Raw Food Feast
2909 Southeast Seventh Avenue
Portland, OR 97206
Stacie Cohen
(503) 771-5605
rawdiva@earthlink.net

Raw Health Network
6410 Southeast Foster
Portland, OR 97206
rawhealth@involved.com

Pennsylvania

Arnold's Way Raw Food Potlucks
319 West Main Street
Lansdale, PA 19446
www.arnoldsway.com

Greenwood Potlucks
Landsdowne, PA 19050
(610) 623-5656

Lancaster Goodness-Alive
1721 Windsor Avenue
Lancaster, PA 17601
Neal Pressley
(717) 397-4448, (717) 575-1862
npress@voicenet.com

Philly Raw & Real
Philadelphia, PA
Ken Shapiro
(215) 677-5817

Pittsburgh Raw Food Group
Pittsburgh, PA
(412) 371-7416
joycekehoe24@yahoo.com

Wellness Network
P.O. Box 267
Wellsboro, PA 16901-0267
(717) 376-3031

Tennessee

Memphis Support Group
Wild Oats at Poplar Avenue
Memphis, TN 38104
Beth Ann Miller
(901) 729-8326, (901) 266-3358

Texas

Austin Live Feast Group
3920 Idalia Drive
Austin, TX 78749
(512) 282-4308
yemiah@livefeast.com
www.livefeast.com

Dallas Raw Experience
Cynthia Beavers
(214) 454-5250
rawfoodchef@aol.com
www.rawheaven.com

Rudra Center for
Enlightened Awareness
609 North Locust Street
Denton, TX 76201
(940) 384-7946

Utah

The Herb Shoppe
160 South State Street
Orem, UT 84058
(801) 224-6900

Virginia

Hampton Roads Living Foods
P.O. Box 3905
Virginia Beach, VA 23454
(757) 422-8645
hrv@ivu.org

Washington

Alexandra's River Inn
4548 Tolt River Road
Carnation, WA 98014
(425) 333-6000, (425) 681-9581
trivia@isomedia.com
www.hometown.aol.com/wheat-
grassjuice/myhomepage/index.html

Friday Night Potluck and Dance
10713 Northeast 117th Avenue
Vancouver, WA 98662
(360) 695-4482

Olympic Peninsula/Port Townsend
Raw Food Support Group
718 A Fir Street
Port Townsend, WA 98368
(360) 385-0126
jespaty@olypen.com

Raw Bellingham Potlucks
(360) 398-1215
kelpguy@islandseaweed.com
rawbellingham@yahoogroups.com

Raw Seattle
10705 Northeast 193rd Street
Bothell, WA 98011
Zita Frederic
(425) 398-1673
rawliving@aol.com
www.rawseattle.org

Wisconsin

Madison Potlucks
Madison, WI
drwilke@shorewoodwellness.com
www.rawmadison.org

Canada

Bob Harrison
Raw-Food Support Group of
Montreal
(514) 739-3830

International Biogenic Society
P.O. Box 849
Nelson, BC V1L 6A5

The Raw House
6386 Street-Denis
Montreal QCH2X3K7
(514) 271-4762
rawvegan@sympatico.ca
www.rawvegan.com

Toronto Potlucks
lisa@at1withnature.com
www.at1withnature.com

Britain

Bionomic Nutrition Forum
www.venusnildram.co.uk/
veganmc/forum.htm

Fresh-Network
P.O. Box 71
Ely, Cambs CB7 4GU
44 870 800 70 70, 44 870 800 70 71
info@fresh-network.com
www.fresh-network.com

Herts Essex Middlessex Position
(Hemp)
63 Leven Drive
Waltham Cross, Herts EN8 8AL
Lisa
01992 624 079

North West London
Fresh Network Group
Paul Moriarty
020 84 51 74 19
justbe@barclays.net

Rawfare
Barnet London
Grant Rowlands
020 844 16252

South West London Fresh
Network Group
Pauline Tilbury
020 86 77 23 29
p.tilbury@freeuk.com

Germany

Brigitte Rondholz
Alte Dorfstr 83
32289 R dinghausen
www.urkostmitbrigitte.de
www.Natuerlichgesund.Net
www.rohmachtfroh.de

Festivals and Events

USA

Essene Gathering
July, Oregon
esseneinfo@aol.com

International Festival of Raw and Living Foods
August, Portland
(503) 246-1684
rawfestival@aol.com

Just Eat an Apple
P.O. Box 900202
San Diego, CA 92190
(800) 205-2350
fred@sunfood.net

Living Now Festival
July, Upstate New York
(716) 858-3631
livingnow@greensunhealing.com
www.greensunhealing.com

Living Nutrition
P.O. Box 256
Sebastopol, CA 95473
(707) 829-0362, (240) 414-5341
www.livingnutrition.com

Rawsome News
P.O. Box 3397
Vista, CA 92085-3397
(619) 260-6968

Rawstock
Raw Passion Productions
P.O. Box 256
Sebastopol, CA 95473
(707) 829-0362
58348-subscribe@zinester.com
www.rawstock.us

SF Life
3640 Garden Bar Road
Lincoln, CA 95648
(415) 751-2806 (sproutline)
sflife@living-foods.com

Australia

Fruitarian News Network
P.O. Box 293
Trinity Beach, QLD 4879
Australia
fruitnet@ozemail.com.au

Real News
P.O. Box 8166
Cairns, QLD 4870
Australia
Fax: 07 4056 31 87
algallo@bigpond.com
www.webspanish-english.com/real-news/

Britain

Fresh Network News
P.O. Box 71
Ely CB7 4GU, UK
+44-0-1353-662849
fresh@karenk.easynet.co.uk
www.fresh-network.com

Germany

International Raw-Food Congress
July, Nürnberg
stephanie.wiegand@roh-leben.de

Spain

Boletin Crudivorismo
49192 La Hiniesta Apartado 186
49080 Zamora, Spain
baltacrudo@yahoo.es

Periodicals and E-Bulletins

Sign up at the website for these emails with information on raw food events and products.

- Loving Foods E-Bulletin, www.lovingfoods.com
- Raw Times, www.rawtimes.com
- Nature's First Law, www.rawfood.com
- Lifefood Nutrition, www.lifefood.com
- Just Eat an Apple, www.justeatanapple.com

Raw and Living Food Retailers

Beverly Hills Juice Club
8382 Beverly Boulevard
Beverly Hills, CA 90048
(323) 655-8300

High Vibe Health and Healing
New York, NY
(212) 777-6645
highvibe.com
Raw food, tools, and product distributor.

Live Live
261 East 10th Street
New York, NY 10009
(212) 505-5504
www.live-live.com
Raw food, tools, and product distributor.

Organic Avenue
23 Ludlow
New York, NY 10002
(212) 334-4593
denise@vegucate.com
Raw food, tools, clothing, and product distributor.

Supersprouts
205 Spadina Avenue
Toronto, Ontario M5T 2C8
Canada
(416) 977-7796
www.supersprouts.com

Raw and Living Food Products

Arnold's Way
319 West Main Street
Store #4 Rear
Lansdale, PA 19446
(215) 361-0116
Offers raw fruit bars mail order.

Blessings Alive
1734 San Pablo Avenue
Berkeley, CA 94702
(510) 527-8916
blessingsalive@hotmail.com
Raw crackers, cookies, and snacks.

Cracker Flax
10 Wallenberg Circle
Monsey, NY 10952
(845) 352-5623
Raw flax crackers.

Crackers Alive
9979 West Lilac Road
Escondido, CA 92026
(760) 749-6881
Dried seed and vegetable crackers.

The Date People
P.O. Box 808
Niland, CA 92257
(760) 359-3212
datefolk@brawleyonline.com
Wide range of dates.

Deep Root Organic
189 ch. de la Riviere, Martinville
Québec JOB 2AO
Canada
(819) 835-9277
biolacto@biolacto.com
www.biolacto.com
Raw cultured vegetables.

Didi's Baking for Health
New York, NY
(212) 505-2232
info@bakingforhealth.com
Dried nut balls and crackers.

Essential Living Foods
(805) 528-4176
www.essentiallivingfoods.com
Olives.

Genesis Juice
Eugene, OR
(541) 344-0967
Live juices freshly pressed daily in glass bottles.

Glaser Organic Farms
19100 Southwest 137th Avenue
Miami, FL 33012
(305) 238-7747
Certified organic farm-grown produce and prepared gourmet raw foods.

Gopal's
29000 Lilac Road
Valley Center, CA 92082
gopalshealthfoods.com
(760) 751-3923
Raw Powerwraps and bars.

Govinda's Raw Power Bar
2651 Ariane Drive
San Diego, CA 92117
(888) 270-0692
Dried snacks and crackers.

Inn of the Seventh Ray
128 Old Topanga Canyon Road
Topanga, California 90290
(310) 455-1311
www.innoftheseventhray.com
Products in health food stores, including patés and sauces.

Living Nutz
(207) 655-5352
wildblueberry@rawfoods.com
Dried, sprouted almond snacks.

Living Tree Community Foods
(800) 260-5534
livingtreecomunity.com
Raw organic nut butters and dried fruits.

Loving Foods
P.O. Box 790358
Paia, HI 96779
(808) 878-8091
allraw@lovingfoods.com
Dried breads, crackers, cookies, bars, and kim chee.

Lydia Kindheart
81 Upland Avenue
Mill Valley, CA 94941
(808) 573-8410
Dried bars and crackers.

Mauk Family Farms
Santa Ana, CA 92075
(714) 547-7977
maukfamilyfarms@cox.net
www.maukfamilyfarms.com
Raw food snacks and products.

Mendocino Sea Vegetable Company
P.O. Box 1265
Mendocino, CA 95460
(707) 937-2050
www.seaweed.net
Wildcrafted sea vegetables.

NHU Foods
P.O. Box 19495
Boulder, CO 80308
(877) 815-6904
Raw and raw dried foods.

Nutiva
P.O. Box 1716
Sebastapol, CA 95473
(707) 823-2800
info@nutiva.com
www.nutiva.com
Raw hemp nuts.

Omega Nutrition
1924 Franklin Street
Vancouver, BC V5L 1R2
Canada
(604) 253-4677
Low-temperature oils.

Rejuvenative Foods
Santa Cruz, CA 95063
(831) 424-3258
Raw nut butters and krauts.

Seed Live Cuisine
17531 Posetano Road
Pacific Palisades, CA 90272
(310) 454-0547
inquires@seedcuisine.com
www.seedcuisine.com
Products in health food stores including patés, sauces, pizzas, and desserts.

Snacks Alive
Santa Cruz, CA
(831) 423-0226
Snack treats.

Sun Organic Farms
(888) 269-9888
Raw seeds, nuts, grains, oils, fruits, and spices.

Raw and Living Food Recipe Books

116 Favorite Tantalizing Good Health Recipes
by Marti Wheeler

Angel Foods
by Cherie Soria

The Complete Book of Raw Food
by various authors

Delights of the Garden
by Imar Hutchins

Dining in the Raw
by Rita Romano

Dry It You'll Like It
by Gen MacManiman

Eating without Heating
by Sergi and Valya Boutenko

Elaina's Pure Joy Kitchen
by Elaina Love

Eydie Mae's Natural Recipes
by E. Hunsburger

Feasting on Raw Foods
by Charles Gerras

The Garden of Eden Raw Fruit & Veggie Recipes
by Phyllis Avery

Get Well Recipes from the Garden of Eden
by V. Bidwell

Gourmet Un Cookbook
by Elizebeth Baker

High Integrity Diet
by Michael Schleyer

Hooked on Raw
by Rhio

Kitchen Garden Cookbook
by Steve Meyrowitz

Life Food Recipe Book
by Annie and David Jubb

Light Eating for Survival
by Marcia Acciardo

Live Food Juices
by H. Kirshner

Living Cuisine
by Renée Underkofler

Living Foods
by George and Dorris Fathman

Living Foods for Optimum Health
by Brian Clement

Living with Green Power
by Elysa Markowitz

Love Your Body
by Viktoras Kulvinskas

The Original Diet
by Karen Whyte

Rainbow Green Live Food Cuisine
by Gabriel Cousens

Raw
by Charlie Trotter and Roxanne Klein

Raw
by Erica Lenkert and Juliano Brotman

Raw Energy Recipes
by L. and S. Kenton

The Raw Food Primer
by Suzanne Alexander Ferrara

Raw Fruit & Veggie Book
by Bircher / Benner

Raw Gourmet
by Nomi Shannon

Rawsome
by Brigitte Mars

The Raw Truth
by Jeremy Safron

Real Soup & Salad Book
by Bernard Jenson

Recipes for a Longer Life
by Ann Wigmore

Recipes for the Now Age
by D. Lampron

Recipes from the Sproutman
by S. Meyrowitz

Rejuvenative Diet
by Dr. J. Christopher

Salt-free Sauerkraut Cookbook
by P. Braggs

Simply Good
by Victoria Bidwell

Soups Alive
by Eleanor Rosenast

Sun Food Cuisine
by Fred Patenaude

Sweet Temptations
by Frances Kendall

Un Cookbook
by Elizebeth Baker

Vibrant Living
by Dr. James Levin

Vital Creations
by Chad Sarno

Warming Up to Living Foods
by Elysa Markowitz and Gabriel Cousens

Books by Subject

Raw Knowledge

Be Your Own Doctor
by Dr. Ann Wigmore

Blatant Raw Foodist Propaganda
by Joel Alexander

Digestion, Assimilation, Elimination & You
by E. Bashaw

Eco Eating
by Sapoty Brook

Enzyme Nutrition
by Dr. Edward Howell

Fruitarianism and Physical Rejuvination
by O.L.M. Abramowski

Fruit the Food and Medicine for Man
by Morris Krok

The Healing Power of Chlorophyll
by Bernard Jenson

The Healing Power Within
by Dr. Ann Wigmore

Heal Your Body
by Dr. Ann Wigmore

Holistic H.E.L.P. Book
by Stanley Kalson

I Live on Fruit
by Essie Honiball and T. C. Fry

In the Beginning God Said Eat Raw Food
by William Scott

Life in the 21st Century
by Victoras Kulvinskas

Living Foods for Radiant Health
by Elaine Bruce

Living Foods Lifestyle
by Brenda Cobb

Metaphysics of Raw Food
by Stella McDermott

Naturama
by Dr. Ann Wigmore

Nature's First Law
by D. Wolfe, S. Arlin, and F. Dinni

Raw Courage World
by Fuad Dinni

Raw Family
by the Boutenkos family

The Raw Food Treatment of Cancer
by Christine Holfi

Raw Kids
by Cheryl Stoycoff

The Raw Life
by Paul Nisson

Raw Power
by Stephen Arlin

Raw Secrets
by Fred Patenaude

Sunfood Diet Success System
by David Wolfe

Survival into the 21st Century
by Victoras Kulvinskas

Books on Foods

Cereal Grasses
by Ronald Seibold

Complete Book of Spices
by Jill Norman

Complete Natural Food Facts
by Sonia Newhouse

Complete Nutritional Food Facts
by Health Research

The Exotic Fruit Book
by Norman Van Aken

A Gourmet's Guide to Fruits
by Louise Steele

A Gourmet's Guide to Mushrooms
by Louise Steele

A Gourmet's Guide to Vegetables
by Louise Steele

Handy Pocket Guide to Tropical Fruits
by Periplus Nature Guides

Herbs & Things
by Jeanne Rose's Herbal

How to Dry Fruit
by Deanna De Long

How to Prune Fruit Trees
by R. Sanford Martin

The New Taste of Chocolate
by Maricel E. Presilla

Sea Green Primer
by Juel Andersons

The Secrets of Spirulina
by Christopher Hills

Sprout for the Love of Everybody
by Victoras Kulvinskas

The Sprouting Book
by Dr. Ann Wigmore

Sprouts
by Esther Munroe

Stalking the Wild Asparagus
by Euell Gibbons

Tropical Fruit
by Desmond Tate

The Wheatgrass Book
by Dr. Ann Wigmore

Wheatgrass Juice
by Betsy Russel Manning

Wheatgrass: Nature's Finest Medicine
by Steve Meyrowitz

Other Really Good Books

The Alchemist
by Paulo Cuelo

Ashtanga Yoga
by Baba Hari Dass

Be Here Now
by Ram Dass

Hope for the Flowers
by Trina Paulus

Illusions
by Richard Bach

The Kin of Ata Are Waiting for You
by Dorothy Bryant

Tools to Enhance Raw Living

Kitchen tools are a blessing to the culinary-minded raw fooder. By having a wide range of tools to work with, you can create gourmet meals to live for. Knowing what kind of equipment is right for you can help obtain the results you want in the kitchen. The right tool is needed for the right job. This section lists common types of tools found in raw food kitchens. Some of the listings have both types and brand names.

Utensils

Household kitchen utensils (bowls, knives, cutting boards, counter tops, spoons, spatulas, and so forth) are made from a variety of substances in our modern age. Some are more ideal than others to work with.

- Glass: A very inert substance great for bowls.
- Ceramic: Natural earthenware, very pure.
- Steel: Very durable and easy to clean.
- Plastic: Can affect the flavor of food, OK for spatulas.
- Wood: Best material for all utensils/great for flavor.
- Aluminum: Extremely toxic. Watch out!

Juicers

Juicers are machines used to separate pulp and juice.

- Centrifugal: Any juicer that has a spinning blade.
- Press: A juicer that ruptures the cells from within.
- Masticating: A juicer that grinds and presses.
- Triturating: A twin-gear juice press.

Recommended Brands

- Miracle: A nice stainless centrifugal juicer.
- Champion: Masticating juicer good for homogenizing.

- Norwalk: A hydraulic press used to produce a juice that is nonoxidizing and lasts the longest of all.
- Juice Man: A very easy-to-use centrifugal juicer.

Blenders

Blenders are used to grind food into liquids.

- Vitamix: A superpowered blender that can blend dry or wet and grind almost anything into liquid. The carafe is eight cups (most blenders are five cups).
- Osteriser: A common household blender that has small blending jars that attach for small portions.
- Multispeed: Any blender that has a variety of speeds.
- Dual speed: A blender with high and low settings.

Sprouting Equipment

Sprouting can be accomplished in a number of ways. Having the tools that work with your lifestyle and kitchen make it much easier to keep a continual sprout garden in your home.

- Jars: Half-gallon glass Ball or Mason jars are best.
- Lids: Look for plastic sprouting lids that screw on.
- Screen: Use nylon screen, which is cheap and easy to find.
- Trays: Plastic trays are available at gardening stores.
- Soil: Garden stores sell organic soil, or use soil from your yard.
- Mistoponic: An automatic sprouting system.
- Biosta: An easy-to-use multitiered sprouting system.

Garnishing Tools

Garnishing adds an element of beauty to any meal. Many master chefs from the Orient can produce huge arrays of garnishes using any type of food available.

- Spiralizer: A tool for making long, curly thin strips of vegetables—as thin as angel hair pasta.

- Carving tools: Small knives and curved blades used to cut fruits and veggies into shapes.
- Zester: A tool for making thin strips of citrus rind.
- Pastry bag: Used to decorate cakes, writing with icing.

Food Processors

Used to grind food into powder or paste or just to mix.

- Cuisinart: This solid standard comes in a variety of sizes. This machine is a true workhorse.
- Krupps: Makes an excellent mini-processor.
- Generic: Good for light grinding, often breaks easily.

Culturing

Used for creating an ideal environment for living bacteria.

- Harsch crock: An earthen jar with a water seal used for making sauerkraut, pickles, and kim chee.
- Tofu press: Used to press water out of soy tofu.
- Seed Cheez Bag: For separating curds and whey.

Dehydrators

Machine for removing water and drying food.

- Harvest Maid: A large dryer good for home use.
- Excalibur: A dryer with a variety of temperature settings, good for both home and commercial applications.
- Cabela's: A great dryer. Glass front, digital timer and settings. Powerful and efficient.
- Stack: Not very efficient, but cheap and easy to obtain.

Glossary

Acidophilus: A type of helpful bacteria used in digestion.

Amylase: A digestive enzyme found in saliva.

Assimilation: The ability to receive nutrients.

Bioactive: Food with its life force.

Biodynamic: A way of organic farming.

Biogenic: Promoting life.

Charge: To induce an electrical current and store it.

Compost: The breakdown of organic materials.

Conventionally grown: Grown with chemical and pesticides.

Cultivated: Grown for the purpose of eating.

Cultured: Food with healthy bacteria living on it.

Dehydrated: Food with water evaporated from it.

Elimination: The expulsion of waste matter from the body.

Enema: A method of cleansing the colon using water.

Enzymes: Substance that split food into its vital parts.

Evaporate: To remove water by using warmth.

Exfoliate: Stimulating the skin to release toxins.

Fasting: The removal of something from daily practice.

Fecal mucoid matter: Old material stuck to the colon walls.

Foraging: Finding wild food or questing for food.

Fruit: Any water-rich food surrounding a seed.

Germination: The beginning process of sprouting.

Grain: Any affixed hull seed that grows as a grass.

Herb: Any green plant whose leaves are edible.

Hybrid: Any food that has been bred.

Intention: The focus of positive energy toward a goal.

Macrobiotic: Eating foods grown in the area where you are.

Natural: Doing things in harmony with nature.

Nut: A seed that has a removable shell and grows on trees.

Organically grown: Grown without the use of chemicals.

Papain: A digestive enzyme found in papaya.

Predigested: Easier to assimilate due to living bacteria.

Preparing: Creating a raw food meal.

Remineralize: To introduce organic minerals to water.

Sprout: The young growth of a future plant.

Vegan: No animal products, meat, dairy, egg, and honey-free.

Wild: Produced by nature without any help from man.

Wisdom: Experience (what we do) plus knowledge (what we learn). A true overstanding about some teaching that we can pass on to others to help benefit their life.

New Entries and Corrections

Add yourself or a local living food resource to our guide or join our mailing list by filling out the form below.

Name ______________________________

Address ______________________________

City ____________________ State ________ Zip ________

Phone ________________ Fax ________________

Email ______________________________

Website ______________________________

What section do we list you in?

____

Do you want to join our mailing list? Y/N

Do you want to distribute copies of *Raw Living* in your establishment? Y/N

Do you want to be listed in our next edition of *Raw Living*? Y/N

Send information to:

Loving Foods
P.O. Box 790358
Paia, HI 96779

Email us at: allraw@lovingfoods.com

Loving Foods Catalog

Books

The Fasting Handbook: Dining from an Empty Bowl, $14

The Raw Truth Recipe Book, $20

Charts

Exotic Fruit Chart: $10.00

Food Drying Chart: $7.00

Four Living Food Groups Chart: $7.00

Sprout Chart: $7.00

T-Shirts

Sprout Tank Top: $20.00

Sprout T-shirt: $20.00

Food Products

Bucky Bars, $1.89

Bucky Bars, case of 30, $32.40